SONGS OF STRUGGLE AND PROTEST

Songs of STRUGGLE and PROTEST

EDITED BY
JOHN McDONNELL

THE MERCIER PRESS
CORK AND DUBLIN

First published 1979 by
GILBERT DALTON LTD
Copyright (c) 1979, John McDonnell
This edition 1986
ISBNO 85342 755 5

CONTENTS

EARLY POPULAR STRUGGLES

The Plague, commonly called *The Black Death*, which in 1348 started to kill off a third of the population of England, gave the downtrodden serf labourers an unexpected opportunity of improving their lot. The serfs were able to exploit the shortage of labour resulting from the devastation of the Plague as a means to bargain for wages and better conditions of life. Through their Parliament, the feudal nobility retaliated by passing in 1350 *The Statute of Labourers* which bound workmen and servants to their masters under penalty of imprisonment, and declared: "The old wages and no more shall be given to servants."[1] As the hostility increased against the powerful landowners, many of whom were the bishops and abbots of the medieval church, the labourers formed themselves into an organisation called *The Great Society* which gave their spontaneous militancy the strength of unity. In the course of a few years *The Statute of Labourers* was revised several times, each time introducing severer penalties. In spite of these efforts to perpetuate it, the feudal system of labour began to break down as more and more serfs went to the towns or joined the ranks of wage labourers in other areas. In 1377 the Statute declared: "They (the wage labourers) do menace the ministers of their lords in life and member, and which is more, gather themselves in great routs and agree by such confederacy that one should aid the other to resist their lords with strong hand, and much other harm they do in sundry manner to the great damage of their said lords and evil example to others."[2]

In 1381 the peasants rose in armed revolt against the imposition of high taxes. Such was the strength of their united effort that, under the leadership of Wat the Tyler and John Ball, a priest, they were able to enter London unopposed where they were met by King Richard II in person, who promised to fulfil all their demands. These promises, however, were not made to be kept and, after murdering Wat The Tyler, the feudal nobility took a bloody revenge on the insolent peasantry who had given them such a fright. Hundreds of peasants were executed, but even if the rising had not the success that at first seemed so certain, the hated Poll Tax was taken off the backs of the working people.

The voice of the oppressed medieval serf could quickly be stifled with the hangman's rope if he uttered seditious ideas.

Today the texts which express the authentic accents of these desperate and defiant people are rare indeed. In the words of John Ball to the peasants of Essex we can catch something of the quality of wary secrecy and ominous determination of this revolutionary movement. "John Shepherd, one time Priest of St. Mary's of York and now of Colchester, greets well John Nameless and John the Miller and John the Carter, and bids them beware of deceit in the town, and stand together in God's name; and bids Piers Plowman go to his work and chastise well Hob the Robber; and take with you John Trueman, and all his comrades, and no more besides, and elect for yourselves one leader and no more . . ."[3]

It was John Ball who preached a sermon to his army of rebellious peasants on a text of his own composition:

> "When Adam delved and Eve span,
> Who was then the gentleman?"

"Good friends, matters cannot go well in England until all things be held in common; when there shall be neither vassals nor lords; when the lords shall be no more masters than ourselves".[4]

The wariness cloaking a mounting anger comes across clearly in *The Cutty Wren* (page 52) where the oppressive enemy is symbolised by the Wren, the King of all Birds. The shepherd who sang this song to Miss Dorothy Blunt, the folk song collector in this century, did not know that it originated in the rising of the peasants in the 14th century, but according to A. L. Lloyd: "He banged the floor with his stick on the accented notes and stamped violently at the end of the verses, saying that to stamp was the right way and reminded of the old times."[5]

The Rocks of Bawn (page 53) is another song of an oppressed peasant class. The seizure of 11,000,000 acres of good land from Irish landowners to reward the officers and men of Cromwell's army, by the *Act of Satisfaction* in 1653, sent many Irish men and women to starve on the rocky pastures of Connacht. It was well said of the barren, eroded landscape of the west that it was not possible to grow enough flax there to make a rope to hang a man, or find enough wood to make his coffin, or enough earth to bury him.

The next two songs (pp. 54-55) came from Scotland and

reflect the bitterness felt by the Scots at the defeat of their hopes in the Jacobite Wars; first in 1707 when their own parliament was abolished by means very similar to those used nearly a hundred years later to abolish the Irish Parliament, and secondly after the ill-fated campaign of 1745 to establish Prince Charles Edward Stuart, the young Pretender, on the throne of England, Scotland and Wales. The campaign ended with the defeat of the clansmen — and some Irish troops trained in France — at Culloden, after which savage reprisals were taken on the survivors and the civilian population by General Wade and "Butcher" Cumberland, son of the Hanoverian King of England. In the aftermath of the battle there seems in fact to have been an attempt actually to exterminate sections of the population of the Highlands. Not only were men, women and children slaughtered, often with the utmost brutality, but the highlanders were attacked ruthlessly at their economic base. Goats, cattle, sheep, horses and other livestock were driven off to be sold to merchants and dealers who came from the Lowlands and from England to share in the spoils of victory. All movables were stolen from the houses which were afterwards burned to the ground. "We hang or shoot anyone that is known to conceal the Pretender", said one officer, "burn their houses and take their cattle of which we have got 8,000 head within these few days past".[6]

For this work the Duke of Cumberland was greeted on his return to London by a piece of music composed by Handel, the Court Composer, to the words "See! The Conquering Hero Comes", and doubtless was gratified when his salary was raised from £15,000 a year to £40,000. A rather charming little flower is also named after him; it is called "Sweet William". In Scotland however, there is a weed which bears the rather less complimentary name "Stinking Billy".

Notes

1. A. L. Morton *A People's History of England* p. 118.
2. Ibid p. 121.
3. John Mulgan *Poems of Freedom* p. 17.
4. H. Fagan and R. H. Hilton *The English Rising of 1381* p. 99.
5. A. L. Lloyd *Folk Song in England* p. 96.
6. John Prebble *Culloden*.

THE FRENCH REVOLUTION AND THE TIDE OF REPUBLICANISM

France, for nearly two centuries, has had as its National Anthem a revolutionary song.

In April 1792, Joseph Rouget de Lisle, a young captain of engineers of the French army stationed at Strasbourg, composed this song as a *Chant de Guerre* for the French revolutionary army setting out on its campaign against the two most powerful reactionary states in Europe, Prussia and Austria. It triumphantly caught the mood of exhilaration and revolutionary zeal felt at that time by so many young French men and women which Wordsworth, the English poet then living in France, later recollected in his poem *The Prelude:*

Bliss was it in that dawn to be alive
and to be young was very heaven.

The song soon became very popular and, when sung at a banquet for army volunteers at Marseilles, it was received with such enthusiasm that it was given the name *La Marseillaise,* by which it has been known ever since.

On July 15th 1795, the *Marseillaise* was declared the official National Anthem of France and, after the overthrow of Charles X by Louis Phillipe in 1830, Rouget de Lisle received a state pension. At his funeral in 1836 his coffin was followed to the graveside by thousands of bare-headed workers. The words and music of his song, in the original French and in translation, are given here on page 56.

The French Revolution was the first revolutionary movement with a deliberately international outlook and seeds from it fell in many parts of Europe as well as in America. In Ireland, Wolfe Tone and his comrades of The Society of United Irishmen derived much of their inspiration from it and, from the writings of men like Tom Paine, whose book *The Rights of Man* appeared in Belfast in 1791. There was among the Presbyterians great enthusiasm for the French Revolution of 1789.

The words of the declaration of resolutions taken at the first meeting of the Society in Belfast in 1791 make interesting reading today:

"In the present great era of reform, when unjust governments are falling in every quarter of Europe, when religious persecution is compelled to abjure her tyranny over conscience, when the rights of man are ascertained in theory and that theory substantiated by practice, when antiquity can no longer defend absurd and oppressive forms against the common sense and common interests of mankind, when all government is acknowledged to originate from the people, and to be only so far obligatory as it protects their rights and promotes their welfare; we think it our duty as Irishmen to come forward, and state what we feel to be our heavy grievance, and what we know to be an effectual remedy."[1]

After this tremendous opening sentence, the declaration goes on to make a moving — and at that time realistic — plea for: "The abolition of bigotry in religion and politics, and the equal distribution of the rights of man through all sects and denominations of Irishmen."[2]

Their particular demands were for: 1. Manhood suffrage 2. Equal electoral districts 3. Abolition of the property qualification 4. Annual Parliaments and 5. Payment of members.[3] These demands were subsequently taken up by the Chartist movement in England forty five years later.

On December 3rd 1792, 244 delegates from all over Ireland assembled at the Tailors' Hall in Dublin to draw up a petition to George III demanding that Catholics be restored: "to a position of equality with Protestants".[4] Wolfe Tone accompanied the delegation that took this petition to the King. This led to the passing of the *Catholic Relief Act* (1793) which removed nearly all the oppressive Penal Laws. However in 1794 the Society of United Irishmen, an open organisation pledged to parliamentary reform, was suppressed. The British government feared the political power of a democratic party which would have won the support of the new Catholic voters.

The tide of popular feeling was now running too strongly to tolerate any restraint, and an armed rising with French aid was planned. In a report to the French government Tone wrote that the Presbyterians of Belfast, who shared in the same political disabilities as the Catholics, were: "The most enlightened body of the nation . . . and enthusiastically attached to the French revolution," while "the Catholics are in the lowest degree of misery and want; ready for any change because no change can make them worse."[5]

When a copy of this report fell into the hands of the government, Tone had to leave for the United States from whence he travelled to France.

The French gave the promised aid but both the expeditions

11

to Ireland came to nothing, largely because of adverse weather conditions, and in 1797 an *Insurrection Act* was passed. Martial Law was declared in Ulster, the two United Irishmen papers, *The Northern Star* and *The Press*, were suppressed and many suspected of republican sympathies were flogged, pitch-capped or pressed into the British navy. In January 1798, William Orr, a young Antrim farmer, was hanged at Carrickfergus for administering an illegal oath. Deciding not to wait any longer for foreign aid, the United Irishmen planned an armed rising in the Spring of 1798. Lord Edward Fitzgerald was chosen as commander-in-chief and Henry Joy McCracken, a Belfast businessman, commander for Ulster.

The rebellion which broke out first in Wexford and Wicklow and then in Antrim and Down, at first prospered and the rebel forces under McCracken occupied Antrim town. However the Dublin leaders had been arrested in a sudden swoop by the authorities and after their initial successes the men of Wexford and Wicklow were defeated at Vinegar Hill. In Ulster, McCracken and Henry Munroe were captured and hanged — Munroe outside the door of his shop and McCracken in the Cornmarket, Belfast on July 17th 1798.

Mary McCracken accompanied her brother on his journey to the scaffold. It was to her that McCracken wrote bitterly after the defeat at Antrim: "These are the times that try men's souls — you will, no doubt, hear a great number of stories respecting the situation of this country. Its present unfortunate state is entirely owing to treachery; the rich always betray the poor".[6]

There are two well-known songs which commemorate this remarkable, popular leader, the one given here on page 57 and a plaintive ballad by P. J. McCall, who is perhaps better known for *Kelly the Boy from Killane* and *Boolavogue*.

A Man's a Man for a' that (page 60) is a fine democratic song by Robert Burns and justly belongs to this section for its testimony to the worth of the common man. It expresses the humanitarian spirit of the age of *The Rights of Man*.

From his childhood, Burns had a deep interest in, and love for, the folk-songs and music of Scotland and a large part of his work as a poet was spent in collecting and editing these songs, often gracing them with touches of his own poetic genius.

His short life — he died at the age of 37 — was spent in poverty and hard work, first on his small farm near Dumfries and then, in order to keep his family alive, as an exiseman. In 1795 he sent the song given here to the publisher George Thomson who had brought out *A Select Collection of Original Scottish Airs*, containing 120 songs, some partly and others wholly by Burns. The poet, in the letter accompanying this song, remarked: "A great critic of song says that love and wine are the exclusive themes for song-writing. The following is on neither subject and consequently is no song, but will be allowed, I think, to be two or three pretty good prose thoughts inverted into rhyme."[7]

In spite of living a life of constant poverty and hardship, he refused all payment for his work for George Thomson. "You may think my songs either above or below price, for they shall absolutely be the one or the other." He wrote to Thomson: "In the honest enthusiasm with which I embark in your undertaking, to talk of money, wages, fee hire, etc. would be downright sodomy of the soul!"[8] However, nine days before he died, he was forced to write to Thomson in desperation: "After all my boasted independence, curst necessity compels me to implore you for five pounds. A cruel wretch of a haberdasher, to whom I owe an account, taking it into his head that I am dying, has commenced a process and will infallibly put me into jail. So, for God's sake, send me that sum, and that by return of post. Forgive me this earnestness but the horrors of a jail have made me half distracted. I do not ask all this gratuitously, for upon returning health, I hereby promise and engage to furnish you with five pounds' worth of the neatest song-genius you have seen." After a brief illness he died on 21st July 1796.[9]

Notes

1. James Connolly *Labour in Irish History* p. 57.
2. *'98. Who Fears to Speak?* p. 8.
3. T. A. Jackson *Ireland her own* p. 119.
4. Ibid p. 123.
5. Frank McDermot *Theobald Wolfe Tone and his times* pp. 121, 122.
6. Edna C. Fitzhenry *Henry Joy McCracken* pp. 134, 135.
7. Robert Ford *The Poetical Works and Letters of Robert Burns* p. 251.
8. Ibid p. 212.
9. Ibid p. 257.

"Being aware that I should have to witness scenes of frightful hunger, I provided myself with as much bread as five men could carry, and on reaching the spot I was surprised to find the wretched hamlet apparently deserted. I entered the hovels to ascertain the cause, and the scenes which presented themselves were such as no tongue or pen can convey the slightest idea of. In the first, six famished and ghastly skeletons, to all appearances dead, were huddled in a corner on some filthy straw, their sole covering what seemed a ragged horse cloth, their wretched legs hanging about naked above the knees. I approached with horror, and found, by a low moaning, they were alive — they were in fever, four children, a woman and what had once been a man.

It is impossible to go through the detail. Suffice it to say that in a few minutes I was surrounded by at least two hundred such phantoms, such frightful spectres as no tongue can describe, either from famine or from fever. Their demoniac yells are still ringing in my ears, and their horrible images are fixed upon my brain.

In another case — decency would forbid what follows, but it must be told — I found myself grasped by a woman with an infant just born in her arms and the remains of a filthy sack across her loins — the sole covering of herself and her baby. The same morning the police opened a house on the adjoining lands, which was observed shut for many days, and two frozen corpses were found lying upon the mud floor half devoured by rats".[1]

Thus Nicolas Cummings, an Irish Magistrate, described for the readers of the London Times of December 24th 1846, the horror of the famine then at its height in Ireland. No other single event in Irish history has had such a profound influence on the subsequent history of the country. No one analysed the causes and consequences of it more thoroughly than Karl Marx, or more vigorously proclaimed them. He put it all very succinctly in a speech to the German Workers' Educational Association in London in 1867:

"The agrarian population lived on potatoes and water; wheat and meat were sent to England; the rent was eaten up in London, Paris and Florence. In 1836, £7,000,000 was sent abroad to absent landowners. Fertilisers were exported with the produce and the rent, and the soil was exhausted. Famine

14

often set in here and there, and owing to the potato blight there was a general famine in 1847. A million people died of starvation. The potato blight resulted from the exhaustion of the soil. It was a product of English rule."[2]

There were political leaders such as John Mitchel and Fintan Lalor who urged the people to keep their crops, pay no rent and take steps to prevent the export of food out of the country. However the leadership of the national movement in Ireland at that time were reluctant to attack private property, and partly because of this vacillation and partly because of the exhaustion of the people, an armed rising in 1848 collapsed quickly.

In 1843 three Irishmen — Charles Gavan Duffy, Thomas Davis and John Blake Dillon — founded a newspaper and a political movement called respectively *The Nation* and *Young Ireland*, with the aim of creating a great national awareness, of awakening the spirit of the downtrodden Irish people. One of the most effective aspects of their journalism was to be found in the poetry section of *The Nation*, where verses by themselves and others, "true to the Gaelic ear",[3] gave a ballad history of Ireland. A collection of these poems and songs was published in 1845 under the title *The Spirit of the Nation*. Over a quarter of the book was written by Thomas Davis, the young editor of the paper, who died of scarlet fever at the tragically early age of 31, on September 16th of that year.

Although not a socialist nor in favour of violence as a means of redress, Davis expresses very clearly in "Udalism and Feudalism", one of his most important political writings, the plight of the mass of Irish people.

"Ireland exists and her millions toil for an alien aristocracy; her soil sends forth its abundance to give palaces, equipages, wines, women and dainties to a few thousands, while the people rot upon their native land. What trifling, what madness, what crime, to talk of prosperity from railways and poor-laws, from manufacturing experiments and agricultural societies while the very land — aye! Ireland itself — belongs not to the people, is not tilled for the people! Redress this, and your palliatives will be needless, your projects realised. Leave this unredressed and your "prosperity" plans may amuse or annoy the public, may impede or assist one or other of the foreign parties who alternately afflict us, but cannot make the sick nation well."[4]

William Smith O'Brien typified all that was most ineffective and reactionary in the leadership of *Young Ireland.* He forbade his followers to take grain from the landlords to give to the people, just beginning to recover from the worst famine in Europe for hundreds of years, and refused to allow the felling of trees to be used as barricades against the military, unless the landlords gave permission. Charles Gavan Duffy, whose carriage was surrounded by Dublin workers as he was being brought to Newgate Prison, on being asked did he want to be rescued, replied: "Certainly not."[5] Given such leadership, the rising of 1848 was hardly likely to succeed. John Mitchel and Fintan Lalor, the only men capable of giving real leadership, were arrested also. Mitchel was transported to Van Diemen's Land and Lalor was imprisoned but died soon after his release, which had been secured because of ill-health and a popular petition.

The fine old popular ballad *Skibbereen* (page 61) expresses the bitterness of those dispossessed after the Famine — or the "Starvation" as many preferred to call it — by landlords seeking to clear their estates of unprofitable tenants. More than a million people were replaced by nearly ten million sheep.

"This is a thing unheard of in Europe," said Marx. "The Russians replace evicted Poles with Russians, not with sheep. Only under the Mongols in China was there once a discussion whether or not to destroy towns to make place for sheep."[6]

Thomas Davis' spirited song *The West's Awake* (page 62), fittingly represents the purpose of his work in *The Nation,* to rouse a sleeping and degraded people to a new consciousness of their nationhood.

Notes

1. John Anthony Scott *The Ballad of America* p. 148.
2. Karl Marx and Frederic Engels *On Ireland* p. 141.
3. M. J. McManus *Thomas Davis and Young Ireland* p. 38.
4. T. W. Rolleston *Prose Writings of Thomas Davis* p. 55.
5. James Connolly *Labour in Irish History* p. 103.
6. Karl Marx and Frederic Engels *On Ireland* p. 142.

19th CENTURY REVOLUTIONARY AND DEMOCRATIC MOVEMENTS

The development of industrial machinery and the growth of factories in Britain in the last quarter of the eighteenth century, rather quaintly called "The Industrial Revolution", suddenly put in the hands of the bourgeoisie the means of securing undreamed-of wealth, and equally suddenly turned a whole mass of craft workers, farm labourers and small farmers into a new class, industrial workers. It was this class that Marx prophesied would become a revolutionary force to overthrow the power of capital and wrest state power from the hands of the propertied classes, thus instituting a socialist order of society.

The first formal expression in Britain of the aspirations of this new class, came when in February 1837, the London Working Men's Association drew up a petition which became known as *The People's Charter:*

1. Equal electoral districts
2. Abolition of property qualifications for M.P.'s
3. Universal manhood suffrage
4. Annual Parliaments
5. Vote by ballot-box
6. Payment of M.P.'s

These demands, now part of the normal structure of parliamentary democracy, must have seemed frighteningly radical at a time when only owners of houses with a rateable value of £10 or more might vote.

Thousands of workers endorsed this charter at large meetings all over England and Scotland. Opinion was divided as to what should be done if the Charter were rejected. In the Chartist movement some, like Feargus O'Connor, the Irishman, were in favour of armed insurrection and others refused to discuss or plan for such a possibility. In 1838 the National Convention of the Chartists met in London and a petition was presented to Parliament bearing 1,280,000 signatures — a huge number, considering the total number of electors was only 839,000. On July 12th the petition was rejected and many mass meetings of protest throughout Britain were followed by arrests and police violence. All further meetings were banned. The defiant mood this provoked in many workers is reflected in a Chartist Poster from Ashton-under-Lyne which reads:

"Men of Ashton! Universal bread or universal blood! Prepare your dagger, torch and guns, your pikes and congreve matches, and all march on for bread and blood, for life or death. Remember the cry for bread of 1,280,000 was called a ridiculous piece of machinery. Oh, ye tyrants! Think you that your mills will stand?"[2]

An attempt was made to organise a general strike. The contacts between the Convention and the Trade Unions were, however, insufficient to bring this about. After most of the leaders had been arrested, the Chartist Convention was dissolved on September 12th, a date which marks the end of the first period of Chartist agitation.

The movement revived as the leaders came out of jail and in July 1840 the National Charter Association was formed and a second, more strongly worded petition was drawn up. It compared the amount spent to maintain British royalty with the sorry situation of the poor. It read in part:

"Your petitioners complain that the hours of labour particularly of the factory workers, are protracted beyond the limits of human endurance, and that the wages earned, after unnatural application to toil in heated and unhealthy workshops, are inadequate to sustain the bodily health and supply those comforts which are so imperative after an excessive waste of physical energy...[3]

The words of one Richard Pilling, tried for taking part in a strike in August 1842, vividly substantiate the Chartists' claim:

"The longer and harder I have worked, the poorer and poorer I have become every year, until at last, I am nearly exhausted. If the masters had taken off another 25 per cent, I would put an end to my existence sooner than kill myself working twelve hours a day in a cotton factory, and eating potatoes and salt."[4]

In May 1842 this petition, bearing 3,315,000 signatures, was scornfully rejected by Parliament. Now the Trade Unions joined in and at a conference in Manchester, they called for a general strike to last until the Charter was accepted. The National Charter Association supported this decision, although Feargus O'Connor spoke strongly against it. The strike lasted several months but at last through hunger and repression the workers were forced back to work. Over 1,500 were arrested and many were imprisoned. The collapse of this strike marks the end of the second period of Chartism.

Ernest Jones, close friend and associate of Karl Marx and writer of *The Song of the Lower Classes* (page 63), joined the movement in 1845 during its third and final stage. He stood unsuccessfully as a Chartist M.P. in the General Election of 1847, when Feargus O'Connor was returned as the only Chartist Member of Parliament. In the summer of 1848 he was arrested along with many others, following the drawing-up of yet another petition bearing nearly two million signatures. About 30,000 people assembled on Kensington Common on April 10th 1848 to march to Westminster with the petition. This crowd, however, was dwarfed by the numbers of troops and police mobilised to ensure order and many mass meetings after this were broken up by police and special constables.

Jones was sentenced to two years solitary confinement. On his release in July 1850, he took up the slogan "The Charter & Victory" and on May 3rd 1851 he started publishing a weekly magazine, *Notes to the People*. In the first number he published his epic poem *The New World — a democratic poem*. He had written it in prison and instead of ink, which he had been denied, he used his blood. *The Song of the Lower Classes* was published in *Notes to the People* March 1852.

1848 was a year that witnessed much national and democratic unrest throughout Europe — attempted risings were crushed in Germany, France and Ireland. It also marked the final struggle of the Chartists in Britain.

The National Charter Association can be called the first party of the British working class. Although the Chartists did not win the six original demands of the People's Charter, the working-class as a whole won some important concessions in the passing of the *Mines Act 1842*, the *Factory Act 1844* and *The Ten Hour Day Act 1847*.

In France the working class struck a more dramatic blow for its freedom when on March 18th 1871, after the defeat of France in the Franco-Prussian War, the workers of Paris seized the Hotel de Ville, ran up a red flag and issued a manifesto, part of which read:

"The proletarians of Paris, amidst the failures and treasons of the ruling classes, have understood that the hour has struck for them to save the situation by taking into their own hands the direction of public affairs"[5]

The government ordered its troops to disarm the workers but many soldiers deserted and General Lecomte, having four times ordered the 81st Regiment to fire on an unarmed gathering which included women and children, was himself shot by his own men. Adolphe Thiers, at the head of his government, fled to Versailles leaving Paris in the hands of its people. Following a General Election the General Council of the Commune was proclaimed in Paris on March 26th.

Its first measures were to disband the army, set up a people's militia and make the police force responsible to the Commune. All Councillors of the Commune were elected by universal suffrage and were recallable by the electorate. Magistrates were also elected and similarly recallable. They and all officials of the Commune were only paid workmen's wages. The Commune passed measures decreeing equal political and social rights for women, decrees on the protection of labour, the abolition of rent and job-placement; it turned over all factories abandoned by their owners to workers' co-operatives. "It was essentially a working-class government," wrote Karl Marx, "the product of the struggle of the producing against the appropriating class, the political form at last discovered under which to work out the economic emancipation of labour."[6]

Attempts to establish similar Communes in Lyons and Marseilles were quickly crushed by the Thiers government. All prisoners captured by government troops were summarily shot, in spite of Thiers' promise that with surrender "chastisement will be arrested at once by an act of peace, excluding only the small number of criminals."[7] Worse was to follow, however, when the Paris Commune was drowned in its own blood.

After eight days of fighting, the forces of the Commune were defeated by the superior might of the government forces. The frightful massacre of men, women and children by the Versailles troops is recorded by many eye-witnesses. Many thousands were slaughtered and in their rush to kill and bury the Commune the troops neglected the elementary decency of ensuring their victims were in fact dead when thrown into the mass graves. It is estimated that about 30,000 Parisians were shot in the capture of Paris and about 45,000 were arrested to be subsequently shot or imprisoned. "Now," said Thiers with some satisfaction, "we have finished with socialism for a long time."[8]

The weakness of the Communards' experiment was that they did not follow up their initial successes, by seizing control of the banks and marching on Versailles to overthrow the Thiers government which had thus an opportunity of recovering its strength to strike back. These lessons about the necessity of capturing state power were well learned later by other revolutionaries, as well as the necessity for a mass party of the working class to prepare the way for revolution. Despite these failures the Paris Commune was nevertheless an important landmark in the development of social democracy, as an attempt "to abolish that class property which makes the labour of the many the wealth of the few".[9]

The Internationale, (page 64), has come to be regarded as the anthem of all progressive humanity, with its call for fraternal bonds between all suffering peoples and classes. A newly independent African country, Congo-Brazzaville, has taken it as its national anthem. Eugene Pottier, who wrote it, was a Communard who escaped the savage reprisals and fled to London. There have been many translations. Two English ones were made by two Scottish comrades of James Connolly in the Social Democratic Federation, the Reverend Dr. Wiglasse and John Leslie. One popular translation begins:

Arise, ye prisoners of starvation
Arise, ye wretched of the earth
For Justice thunders condemnation
A better world's in birth.[10]

The song was set to music by Pierre Degeyter.

Another member of the Social Democratic Federation wrote *The Red Flag*, (page 66), a song that has for years been the battle hymn of the British Socialist movement and is sung at the close of every British Labour Party Conference. Jim Connell born in 1852 at Killskyre, Co. Meath, member at an early age of the Fenian Brotherhood, member of the Executive of the Land League in Britain where he spent most of his life, member of the Social Democratic Federation and later of the Independent Labour Party, was its author. The big Irishman once described himself as "a sheep farmer, dock labourer, navvy, railway-man, draper, journalist, lawyer of sorts and all the time a poacher."[11] His illegal activities served him well in the writing of two books, *The Confessions of a Poacher* and *The Truth about the Game Laws*, as well as in the composition of a spirited song *The Old Poacher's Song*, published in *Red Flag Rhymes*, the opening verse of which runs:

In boyhood I quaffed with a passionate love
The breath of the mountain and moor
And hated the greed of the covetous lord
Who fenced out the weak and the poor;

And later through covert and pheasant-stocked glade
I swept like the blast of the north
I broke ev'ry law that the land robbers made
And mocked at the strength they put forth.[12]

The Red Flag was first published in 1889 in the Christmas issue of the S.D.F. paper *Justice*. Jim Connell told his friend Tom Mahn that he was "inspired by the Paris Commune, the heroism of the Russian nihilists, the firmness of the Irish Land Leaguers, the devotion unto death of the Chicago anarchists." About the tune for it, he wrote: "On the night I wrote the song I was returning from a lecture by Herbert Burrows. He spoke as if socialism was his religion. This inspired me to write it. The only tune that ever has or ever will suit *The Red Flag* is the one I hummed when I wrote it — I mean *The White Cockade*. A. S. Headingly took it on himself to change the tune. May God forgive him, for I never shall! He linked the words with *Maryland*, the proper name of which is *Tannenbaum*, an old German Roman Catholic hymn."[13] It is, in fact, an old Christmas carol — 'tannenbaum' being the German for fir-tree or Christmas tree.

A poem entitled *The Red Flag* by a chartist poet, Alfred Fennell, published in *The Democratic Review*, 1850, may have influenced Jim Connell. It starts:

Tis in the Red Flag true republicans glory;
Red is the emblem of Justice and Right —
By martyrs' blood dyed, whose names live in story,
The victors, though fallen in liberty's fight.
Fast flow our tears for the fetter'd and slaughter'd,
And exiles who wander o'er valley and crag.
Too long has the earth by tyrants been tortured.
They shall crouch yet and cower, before our red flag.[14]

Jim Connell died at the age of seventy-seven on February 8th 1929.

Notes

1. R. G. Gammage *History of the Chartist Movement* 1837-1854 p. 6.
2. A. L. Morton and George Tate *The British Labour Movement 1770-1920* p. 86.
3. Ibid p. 91.
4. Ibid p. 92.

22

5. Karl Marx and Frederic Engels *On the Paris Commune* p. 68.

6. Ibid p. 75.

7. Ibid p. 88.

8. V. I. Lenin *Lessons of the Commune and in memory of the Commune* p. 12.

9. Marx and Engels *Op. Cit.* p. 75.

10. Gemkow Heinrich *Karl Marx* p. 332.

11. *News Chronicle* 23rd March 1937.

12. Jim Connell *Red Flag Rhymes* p. 19.

13. John A. Yates *Pioneers to Power* p. 114.

14. Juri V. Kovalyov *An Anthology of Chartist Literature* p. 130.

INDUSTRIAL LIFE AND THE GROWTH OF TRADES UNIONS

The songs of workers composed and sung sometimes in the workplace itself, are obviously markedly different in character from the poems and anthems composed by socialists who have had little or no direct experience of manual labour. The vocabulary and imagery of these songs come from lives closely moulded by a harsh daily routine and daily struggle for a livelihood and very, very rarely are the grand abstract words such as *liberty, equality, fraternity* to be found in their lines. They express the feelings of individual men and women or groups of workers about particular incidents and people, funny or sorrowful, angry or happy.

The Coal-owner and The Pitman's wife, (page 67), a small masterpiece, has been described by A. L. Lloyd as "wearing a smile that shows strong teeth."[1] It dates from the Durham strike of 1844 and was written by a collier, William Hornsby of Shotton Moor. Since it was discovered again in 1951 by another miner, J. S. Bell of Whiston, and published in Lloyd's *Come all ye bold Miners,* it has become very popular. The mining industry has been particularly noted for its fine songs. Probably the harshness and isolation of the conditions of work, and the danger which fostered the spirit of comradeship among the miners, have contributed to this creativity.

The greatest songwriter among miners must surely be Tommy Armstrong born in 1848 who started work at the age of nine and spent most of his long working life at Tanfield Lea. He sold his songs, printed on broadsheets, around the pubs to raise drinking money. "Me dad's muse was a mug of ale,"[2] remarked one of his fourteen children. Besides this sociable characteristic, however, he had a real sense of responsibility to the miners, amongst whom he was known as "Tommy the Poet" for his songs in their Northumbrian dialect, and felt a deep obligation to record the landmarks in their history. "When ye're the pitman's poet and looked up to for it, wey! if a disaster or a strike goos by wi'oot a song fre ye, they say 'What's wi' Tommy Armstrong? Has someone druv a spigot in him an' let 'oot aal the inspiration?'"[3] Although he could not sing himself, he formed a concert party in which, with the aid of disguises and his quick wit, he entertained at concerts given to raise money for the victims of pit disasters, for strike funds, for reading rooms and for the miners' union.

He is one of the best of all worker poets and A. L. Lloyd has described his work as "characterised by a profound class consciousness and a notable faculty for criticism of society."[4] Most of Armstrong's strike ballads were made during the 1880's and 1890's which was a period of great militancy and industrial struggle.

The membership of "The Miners Federation of Great Britain," formed in 1889, had risen by the year 1900 from 36,000 to 147,000. This demonstrates the enormous increase in Trade Union consciousness amongst the workers during the decade. The struggle, on which *The Durham Lockout*, (page 68), is based, began in March 1892. A fall in coal prices had led the Durham colliery owners to propose a 10% reduction in wages. The miners refused and were locked out. With their families starving, the men agreed after six weeks to accept the wage-cut. Immediately the owners demanded a 13½% cut. It was at this point that Armstrong's ballad was written and used to collect funds. The men rejected the 13½% cut and the lock-out continued until eventually the owners agreed to operate a 10% cut. Armstrong died at Tantokie on the 20th August 1920, aged seventy-two.

As early as 1729 the British Parliament passed laws, applying with equal force to Ireland, called the *Anti-Combination Acts*, which effectively prevented the formation of Trade Unions. In 1743 Parliament prohibited assemblies of "three or more persons for the purpose of making bye-laws respecting journeymen, apprentices or servants"[5] This law further banned the collecting of money for the support of unemployed journeymen and made innkeepers who allowed their premises to be used for Trade Union meetings liable to a fine of £20 for each offence. In July 1800 the most severe *Combination Act* was rushed through the British Parliament in the reactionary fervour provoked by the French Revolution. It prohibited every kind of combination; offenders would be brought before any magistrate and were liable to three months imprisonment. One clause compelled the accused, under severe penalties, to give evidence against themselves. In *The Town Labourer* J. L. and Barbara Hammond write: "Joseph Sherwin of Stockport, where the average wage was eight shillings a week for fourteen hours a day, gave a case of a master in a steam-loom factory in 1816, who reduced wages 3d a loom for artificial light, i.e. a reduction of 6d to most, to some few 9d; the master forgot to return the reduction in summer, and when winter came again (1817) he wanted to make a fresh reduction; the workers objected and left work, twelve women and eleven men. They were taken before the magistrate who sent them out into the yard to deliberate whether they would go to work or to prison. They refused to return at the reduced price, and were given a month's imprisonment, the women at Middlewick and the men at Chester!"[6]

It was in the teeth of such attempts at repression that the Trade Union movement was built. The working class took every opportunity to win concessions from the employers and their Parliament and in 1824 the Combination Acts were repealed. There then followed a great flowering of Trade Union organisation and activity.

The Trade Unions went from strength to strength; wages were pushed up and working hours were pushed down. In 1868 the Trades Union Congress was formed at Manchester. In 1894 the Irish Trade Unions formed their own Congress. By 1871 working hours were being reduced to nine hours a day. It was for a nine hour day that the engineering workers on the north-east coast of England struck in 1871. The strike lasted five months and ended in success. "The Strike," (page 70), was written during this stoppage by Joe Wilson for the engineering workers of W. Armstrong's of Newcastle-on-Tyne.

The darkest aspect of nineteenth-century capitalism is certainly its exploitation of child labour, which it managed strangely to combine with a sentimental attitude to children in general.

The report of the Children's Employment Commission in 1842 found instances where "Children are taken into these mines to work as early as four years of age, sometimes at five, and between five and six, not infrequently between six and seven, and often from seven to eight, while from eight to nine is the ordinary age at which employment in these mines commences."[7] Frederick Engels in his classic study, *The Condition of the Working Class in England,* gives a harrowing account of the exploitation of the labour of women and children in wealthy nineteenth-century Britain: "They are set to transporting the ore of coal loosened by the miner, from its place to the horse-path or the main shaft, and to opening and shutting the doors (which separate the divisions of the mine and regulate its ventilation) for the passage of worker and material. For watching the doors the smallest children are usually employed, who thus pass twelve hours daily in the dark, alone, sitting usually in damp passages without even having work enough to save them from the stupefying, brutalising tedium of doing nothing. The transport of coal and iron-stone, on the other hand, is very hard labour, the stuff being shoved in large tubs, without wheels, over the uneven floor of the mine, often over moist clay or through water, and frequently up steep inclines and through paths so low-roofed that the workers are forced to creep on hands and knees. For this more wearing labour, therefore, older children and half-grown girls are employed. One man or two boys per tub are employed, according to circumstances; and, if two boys, one pushes and the other pulls.

The children and young people who are employed in transporting coal and iron-stone all complain of being over-tired. Even in the most recklessly conducted industrial establishments there is no such universal and exaggerated over-work.

It is constantly happening that children throw themselves down on the stone hearth or the floor as soon as they reach home, fall asleep at once without being able to take a bite of food and have to be washed and put to bed while asleep. It even happens that they lie down on the way home and are found by their parents late at night asleep on the road."[8]

The work of separating lead ore from gravel was a job assigned to children and old or infirm miners. This gave rise to the expression "a miner's second childhood." *Fourpence a day*, (page 71), is a song about the children engaged in this work.

The feeling of bitterness felt by the mineworker in *The Banks of the Dee*, (page 72), rejected by his employers because at fifty-six he's considered too old to work, is shared by many displaced and unemployed workers. The poignant song is on the one hand a protest and a warning to young piece workers on the dangers of over-production. The warning is compounded in the popular wood-turners' song *William Brown*, (page 73).

The farm labourer was engaged in a struggle as hard and unrelenting as the miner or industrial worker. Their union, The National Agricultural Labourers' Union, founded by Joseph Arch in 1872 had a membership of 10,000 by the beginning of 1873. Arch, who devoted his whole life to the cause of the farm labourers, wrote in his autobiography: "We labourers had no lack of lords and masters. There was the parson and his wife at rectory; there was the Squire, with his hand of iron over-shadowing us all. At the sight of the Squire the people trembled. He lorded it right feudally over his tenants, the farmers; the farmers then tyrannised over the labourers; the labourers were no better than toads under a harrow.

"Some of the farmers' wives were in sympathy with the people, but only a very few of them. I wish I could say as much for their husbands. What kindliness they possessed was like the other side of the moon in relation to the earth; it was always turned away from the agricultural labourer.

"They impressed themselves on me as task-masters and oppressors, and my heart used to burn within me when I heard of their doings, and when I saw how the men who toiled so hard for them were treated like the dirt beneath their feet."[9]

Joesph Arch was twice elected Liberal M.P. before he retired from Parliament in 1900. He died in 1919 aged 92.

Notes

1. A. L. Lloyd *Folk Song in England* p. 330.

2. Ibid p. 359.

3. Ibid p. 378.

4. Quoted in Gilfellon *Tommy Armstrong Sings* p. 5.

5. Andrew Boyd *The Rise of the Irish Trade Unions* p. 8.

6. J. L. and Barbara Hammond *The Town Labourer 1760-1832* p. 130.

7. Quoted in Lionel Birch *The History of the T.U.C. 1868-1968* p. 22.

8. *The Condition of the Working Class in England* by Frederic Engels in Marx and Engels *On Britain* p. 280-281.

9. Quoted by Roy Palmer *The Painful Plough* p. 22.

THE FIGHT AGAINST EXPLOITATION — INDUSTRIAL AND RACIAL

The vast industrial power that the U.S.A. represents today is often attributed to the initiative and vision of the entrepreneurs who exploited the resources of the New World. Not so often mentioned in the official histories are the labours of the millions of immigrant workers who built this El Dorado and payed for it with their blood, lives and the lives of their families.[1]

The bitter consciousness of the need for combining and organising was forced on the labourers by many hard lessons. The difficulties of organising a working class divided, not only by skills and the traditional obstacles to unity, but also by race and language, were very considerable. It was an aspiration to a unity that would transcend national, cultural and craft differences that brought the organisation called the Industrial Workers of the World into being in 1905. The constitution it adopted in Chicago in January of that year was openly critical of capitalism. "The system offers", the document declared, "only a perpetual struggle for slight relief within wage slavery. It is blind to the possibility of establishing an industrial democracy, wherein there shall be no wage slavery but where the workers will own the tools which they operate and the product of which they alone will enjoy."[2]

Although its aims were political, the IWW was not prepared either to enter the political arena itself, or affiliate with a political party that would. In essence it was syndicalist and the following quotation from its constitution can stand as a complete definition of syndicalist aims: "The growth and development of this organisation will build up within itself the structure of an industrial democracy — a workers co-operative republic — which must finally burst the shell of capitalist government and be the agency by which the working people will operate the industries and appropriate the products to themselves."[3]

James Connolly was an organiser for the IWW during his years in America and Jim Larkin was also closely associated with it. Another outstanding personality in the IWW was William "Big Bill" Haywood. In his autobiography he writes about the political role of the IWW:

"The history of the IWW has shown the significance of political action. While there are some members who decry legislative and congressional action and who refuse to cast a ballot for any political party in America, yet the IWW has fought more political battles for the working class than any other organisation or political party in America. They have fought against vagrancy laws, against criminal syndicalism laws, and to establish the right of workers to organise. They have gone on strike for men in prison."[4]

The IWW suffered much persecution and harassment by the authorities. In the infamous Chicago trials, 93 members were charged under the criminal conspiracy laws, convicted and condemned to prison sentences which totalled more than 818 years and fined sums of money amounting to £2,570,000. In 1912 at Lawrence, Massachussetts, two young textile workers, a girl and a boy, part of a crowd of strikers protesting against a reduction in wages, were killed by police, the boy stabbed with a bayonet and the girl shot. Although nineteen witnesses swore they had seen the police officer shoot the girl, Anna La Piza, two strike leaders, both members of the IWW were charged with being accessories to the crime.

They were however acquitted. Apart from death and imprisonment, deportation was used as a weapon against the organisation. Jim Larkin was deported in 1923.

Ralph Chaplin wrote *Solidarity Forever*, (page 76), one of the most famous working-class songs, in 1915. He was a member of the IWW and, like Joe Hill, was a frequent contributor to the IWW song book. This song goes to the tune of *John Brown's Body*.

The struggle in the U.S. between the workers and the employers was often waged with incredible ferocity. A particularly atrocious crime, *The Ludlow Massacre*, (page 78), is commemorated here in a ballad by Woody Guthrie, the greatest balladeer the American labour movement has ever produced. It tells of the strike mounted in September 1913 against the Colorado Iron and Fuel Co. owned by John D. Rockerfeller, when thousands of workers of Greek, Slav, Italian and Mexican descent were turned out of the company's shanty town and took shelter in tent encampments. A Colorado congressman, Keating, described the conditions of life in the district:

"Industrial and political conditions in Las Animas and Huerfano counties have for many years been a menace and a disgrace to our state. For more than ten years the coal companies have owned every official in both counties. Last fall they lost the district judge and district attorney, but that has been their sole defeat. Businessmen who have dared to protest have been prosecuted and in many cases driven out. The administration of law has been a farce. As an example: hundreds of men have been killed in the Southern Colorado coal mines during these ten years, yet no coroner's jury, except in one case, has returned a verdict holding the companies responsible, the blame being placed on the dead miner."[5]

The strike lasted eight months, through the winter and into the spring. In April 1914, Adjutant-General Chase organised two companies of the National Guard and on April 20th sent them into the tent towns. All day the gunmen fired into the tents, where the occupants lay in trenches dug when it was heard that the troopers were coming. At nightfall they tried to escape in the darkness but the soldiers set fire to the tents. When the firing stopped 21 people lay dead; 13 were children and 2 were women. Louis Tikxas, one of the mine workers' leaders, and three other miners, were captured and murdered in cold blood by the militiamen.

The story of the struggle of black Americans for equal status with whites is one that has received considerable attention, particularly when it throws a flattering light on some benevolent white liberator such as Abraham Lincoln. However, the racial question ought not to be separated from the class struggle, of which it is a part — although sometimes not easily seen as such. The heavier exploitation of some on the grounds of race or colour does not lighten the burden of exploitation on the rest; it maintains it.

Black Americans have a longer history of struggle against oppression than any other groups in the U.S. The black slave could never integrate with the white settler society like subsequent white immigrants could and did. He remained on the lower levels of a society that would only accept him as servant or clown and in a country to which his parents had not wished to be brought. Their struggle ranges from the days when the issue was the relatively simple one of the abolition of slavery, to today when it is a question of civil rights and the Black Power Movement.

As recently as 1958 James Wilson, a black porter, was sentenced to death for stealing $1.75, a sentence which on appeal was commuted to life imprisonment! This illustrates the type of racist attitude in the U.S. which has distorted legality and has bred a generation of young black men and women who want to sever all connections between themselves and white society. No less outrageous than the case of

James Wilson was that of George Jackson in 1961. At 18 he was involved in a robbery where $70 were stolen. He received an indeterminate sentence that could range from one year to life. Seven of his eleven years in prison were spent in solitary confinement but he spent them profitably in reading and study. He became a highly articulate revolutionary and many of the hundreds of letters he sent to his family from prison have been published in a stirring book *Soledad Brother,* a classic of prison literature.

The black people of America have contributed music and song of great beauty and power to western culture. Their long struggle against slavery and oppression gave birth to some of the best literature of protest to be found in the world. The life of Frederick Douglass is a stirring testimony to the worth of man. Born a slave in 1817 he succeeded in escaping and became an active worker in the Anti-Slavery Movement. As a boy he had gained access to an elementary school reader and taught himself to read. Amongst his subsequent writings are his famous autobiographies. He was inspired to escape by the song *Run to Jesus* (page 77). The black people did not accept slavery with submission, many escaped north from the southern states. Herbert A. P. Theker in his book *Negro Slave Revolts In The United States,* records over 250 slave insurrections. Frederick Douglass was editor of the newspaper *The Northern Star.* A great orator, he once said: "Who would be free, themselves must strike the blow."[8] When he issued his call to his people to take arms to win their freedom and smash slavery in the southern states, there was a great response. About 180,000 black Americans served as soldiers, 25,000 as navy personnel and about 250,000 as workers for the armed forces. Their contribution was decisive. The powerful song *Oh! Freedom,* (page 80), dates from the civil war period where it was used as a marching song by black regiments.

Notes

1. *Journal of Irish Labour History Vol. 1. No. 1.* p. 42.
2. William D. Haywood *The Autobiography of Big Bill Haywood* p. 176.
3. Ibid p. 179.
4. Ibid p. 222.
5. John Greenway *American Folksongs of Protest* p. 151.
6. Angela Davis *If they come in the morning* p. 141.
7. Ibid p. 197.
8. Bradford Chamber and Rebecca Moon *Right On* p. 159.

JOE HILL — THE MAN WHO NEVER DIED

Joe Hill, the author of many songs in the IWW songbook, was born on October 7th 1879 in Graule, Sweden. In 1902 he and his brother emigrated, like many fellow Swedes, to America. He worked at many different jobs and during that time changed his name from Joel Hagglund to Joseph Hillstrom, which his friends shortened to Joe Hill. In 1910 he joined the IWW or "Wobblies" as they were known. He soon became the most popular of the song-writers associated with the IWW and many of his songs were printed in the IWW songbook, *The Little Red Song Book*, which had as its subtitle *Songs to fan the flames of discontent*. He dedicated the remainder of his short life to the working-class and the IWW. He was a frequent speaker at IWW meetings and an organiser in the movement.

In 1911 and 1912, the State of Utah was the scene of many bitter struggles on labour issues and on the issue of free speech. In the summer of 1913 the IWW led a successful strike against one of the biggest companies in the State, The Utah Construction Co.. Joe Hill participated in this strike of railway construction workers which won a wage increase of 25% and a reduction of daily hours from ten to nine. Thereafter IWW-organised meetings would be broken up by thugs hired by The Utah Construction Co. and The Utah Copper Co. and Wobbly leaders would be charged with inciting to riot.

At 9.45 p.m. on Saturday January 10th 1914, two armed men entered Morrison's grocery store in Salt Lake City and said "We've got you now."[1] Whereupon they shot Morrison, a retired police officer, and his son Arling who tried to resist with a gun. The son died instantly and the father some hours afterwards without giving any clue about the murders.

The same night at about 11.00 o'clock Joe Hill was treated by a doctor, six miles from the store, for a bullet wound. Three days later the doctor, while treating him, gave him a drug which led to his easy arrest. While he was resting in his room the police burst in and shot him in the hand. For three days he lay seriously ill in jail and was then charged with the murders committed in the store.

He told the doctor who had treated him that he had received the wound in a quarrel with another man over a girl. To protect this woman Joe Hill would not allow her name to be mentioned throughout his trial, nor would he give any further details of how he was wounded. The fact that he was shot was the only evidence the State had to hold him for trial, and indeed after his trial the Board of Pardons offered him his freedom if he would explain the circumstances of his receiving the wound.

The local newspapers immediately presumed him guilty and conducted a hate campaign against Joe Hill and the IWW. There had been unsolved murders in the area and they were determined to find someone guilty. Joe Hill provided them with an ideal scapegoat and when it was discovered he was a Wobbly it only added to their determination. Some curious aspects of the case did not receive much publicity in the newspapers. The store keeper, an ex-policeman, told his wife he had enemies. A few days before his death he told a police captain that he was in constant dread of people he had arrested and regretted ever having been in the police force. Several other suspects were arrested, including one with a bloodstained handkerchief but all were released. None of the State witnesses identified Joe Hill. The doctor testified that the bullet that hit Joe went right through him but no bullet mark or bullet was found in the store. Between the preliminary hearing and the trial most of the witnesses changed their testimony. When this was noticed the records of the preliminary hearing were asked for and were found to have disappeared. Hill had no motive to commit the murders and becoming dissatisfied with his lawyers he attempted to discharge them. The judge would not allow this.

Joe Hill did not want the IWW to be involved in the case and said that money needed for organisational work should not be diverted for his defence. "If my life will help some other working man to a fair trial," he said, "I am ready to give it. If by giving my life I can aid others to the fairness denied me, I have not lived in vain."[2]

After his conviction many prominent people and organisations tried to help him. Among these was the Swedish Minister in the U.S., W. A. F. Ekengren, who intervened and called for a new trial. With the support of his government, he did all in his power to secure the release of Joe Hill. He appealed to the American president Woodrow Wilson who ordered a stay of execution. Joe Hill's appeal to the Board of Pardons was then rejected and President Wilson again intervened and tried to impress on the Governor of Utah "the justice and desirability of a thorough re-consideration of the case of Joseph Hillstrom."[3] This and all the other appeals were rejected.

During his last day alive Joe Hill wrote letters and telegrams. To his friend and fellow worker, Elizabeth Gurley Flynn, he wrote: "Composed new song last week with music dedicated to the 'Dove of Peace.' It's coming, and now goodbye, Gurley dear, I have lived like a rebel and I shall die like a rebel."[4] To the trade-union organiser, Big Bill Haywood, he wrote: "Good-bye Bill, I die like a true rebel. Don't waste any time mourning — organise! It is a hundred miles from here to Wyoming. Could you arrange to have my body hauled to the State line to be buried? I don't want to be found dead in Utah."[5]

The reporter from the *Salt Lake Herald — Republican*, who interviewed him the night before his execution, wrote of his self-possession and lack of nervousness. His natural sense of humour had not left him and he seemed possessed of a spirit of confidence and optimism. When the reporter asked him what disposition he was going to make of his effects, trinkets and personal belongings, Hill replied that he had nothing to dispose of and had never believed in such things. "But I have a will to make," he said, "and I'll scribble it. I'll send it to the world in care of Ed. Rowan and my IWW friends."[6] He then sat down on his cot and wrote the song, *My Will*, (page 81).

The next morning at 7.42 a.m., strapped to a chair like Connolly, Joe Hill was judicially murdered with four bullets. At the funeral his memorial card read: "In memoriam Joe Hill. We never forget. Murdered by the State of Utah, November 19th, 1915."

Jim Larkin, who was in America at the time, speaking at his funeral, said: "Joe Hill was shot to death because he was a member of the fighting section of the working class, the IWW. Over the great heart of Joe Hill, now stilled in death, let us take up his burden, re-dedicate ourselves to the cause that knows no failure, and for which Joseph Hillstrom cheerfully gave his all, his valuable life. Though dead in flesh, he liveth amongst us."[7]

On the first anniversary of his death, November 19th 1916, delegates to the tenth convention of the IWW received the ashes of Joe Hill in small envelopes. These ashes were distributed throughout all the states of the U.S. — with the exception of Utah — and in every country in South America, Europe, Australia and in New Zealand, South Africa and Asia, complying with Joe Hill's last wishes.

There are about two dozen songs by Joe Hill known today. The best are *The Preacher and the Slave, Casey Jones — The Union Scab, We Will Sing One Song, There is Power,* and *Should I Ever Be A Soldier.* Writing in *Solidarity,* on May 22nd 1915, Elizabeth Gurley Flynn declared: "Joe writes songs that sing, that lilt and laugh and sparkle, that kindle the fires of revolt in the most crushed spirit and quicken the desire for fuller life in the most humble slave. He has put into words the inarticulate craving of 'the sailor, and the tailor and the lumberjack' for freedom, nor does he forget 'the pretty girls that's making curls'. He has expressed the manifold phrases of our propaganda from the gay of Mr. Block and Casey Jones to the grave of 'Should a gun I ever shoulder, Tis to crush the tyrant's might'. He has crystallised the organisation's spirit into imperishable forms, songs of the people — folk-songs."[8]

"Casey Jones" is the first known song by Joe Hill and I give it here on page 82. He may have written others before it, but unfortunately they have not survived. This song was written to help railwaymen on the South Pacific line in California who were on strike in 1911. It is a parody of another ballad of the same name, popular at the time, and is sung to the same tune. It was printed on coloured cards the printer happened to have available at the time and was sold both to help the strike fund and to boost morale. Its theme, an attack on the scabs who work during a strike, is as relevant today as it was then.

Joe Hill, (page 84), was written by Alfred Hayes in 1925, on the tenth anniversary of Hill's judicial murder. It was set to music by Carl Robinson. If you are lucky enough you may find a recording of it, sung magnificently by Paul Robeson.

Notes

1. Dr Philip S. Foner *The Case of Joe Hill* p. 18.
2. Dr Philip S. Foner *The Letters of Joe Hill* p. 36.
3. Foner *The Case of Joe Hill* p. 93.
4. Foner *The Letters of Joe Hill* p. 83.
5. Ibid p. 84.
6. Ibid p. 87.
7. Foner *The Case of Joe Hill* p. 98.
8. Barrie Stavis and Frank Harmon *Songs of Joe Hill* p. 4.

"A strike in the tramway would, no doubt, produce turmoil and disorder created by the roughs and looters, but what chance would the men without funds have in a contest with the company who could and would, spend £100,000 or more," boasted William Martin Murphy on the night of the 19th July 1913 to his employees in the Dublin United Tramway Company. He went on to underline the threat of starvation for any who dared step out of line. "You must recollect," he said, "when dealing with a company of this kind that every one of the shareholders to the number of five, six or seven thousands, will have three meals a day whether the men succeed or not. I don't know if the men who go out can count on this."[1]

On August 21st, 1913, Murphy sacked forty men because they were members of the newly formed and rapidly growing Irish Transport and General Workers Union. The greatest labour struggle in the history of Ireland had begun. At 9.40 on Tuesday, August 26th — the beginning of Horse Show Week — the ITGWU called out their men in protest and with a demand for increased wages. A meeting called for O'Connell Street the following Sunday to be addressed by Jim Larkin was proclaimed by the Chief Magistrate of Dublin. A campaign of police violence was mounted against the strikers and on the Saturday night James Nolan died in hospital after being savagely beaten with batons. James Connolly was arrested and given a sentence of three months but, going on hunger strike, he was released after seven days. Jim Larkin turned up to address the proclaimed meeting in O'Connell Street but was arrested and taken away when he had only begun to speak. His arrest was the signal for a fierce baton charge on the bystanders. The uncontrolled savagery visited on the civilians earned for that day the title "Bloody Sunday". Over four hundred people were injured and another man, James Byrne, died in hospital.

That night, and for many nights afterwards, the police entered workers' homes, smashing furniture and delph. "Police swept down from many quarters," wrote an eye-witness of "Bloody Sunday," "hemmed in the crowd and used their heavy batons on anyone who came in their way. I saw women knocked down and kicked. I scurried up a side street. At the other end the police struck people as they lay injured on the ground, struck them again and again. I could hear the crunch as the heavy sticks struck unprotected skulls. I was in favour of the strikers."[2]

On September 3rd the Dublin employers met and agreed to lock out any worker who would not sign the following pledge: "I hereby undertake to carry out all instructions given me by or on behalf of my employers, and further I agree to immediately resign my membership of the Irish Transport and General Workers' Union (if a member) and I further undertake that I will not join or in anyway support this union."[3] Heroically the workers responded to this threat by choosing lock-out rather than allow the ITGWU be smashed. Their class solidarity inspired Connolly to write an article for the Glasgow socialist paper, *Forward*, which he called *Glorious Dublin*. In it he shows his pride in the actions of the Dublin workers. "Baton charges, prison cells, untimely death and acute starvation — all were faced without a murmur, and in face of them all, the brave Dublin workers never lost faith in their ultimate triumph, never doubted that their organisation would emerge victorious from the struggle." Of the heroic women and girls, he wrote: "In every shop, factory and sweating hell-hole in Dublin, as the agreement is presented, they march out with pinched faces, threadbare clothes and miserable footwear, with high hopes, undaunted spirit and glorious resolve shining out of their eyes. Happy the men who will secure such wives; thrice blessed the nation which has such girls as the future mothers of the race! Ah, comrades, it is good to have lived in Dublin in these days."[4]

Full scale battle was now joined, with the employers determined to starve the workers into submission; the workers resisted with every fibre of their strength. Larkin's sister, Delia, and the Countess Markievicz organised soup kitchens in Liberty Hall. Mass meetings of support were held in Britain and the British Trade Union movement contributed large sums of money. This aid came in the form of foodships sent to Dublin. There was splendid solidarity from the British working-class but the trade-union leaders would not back sympathetic strike action as requested by Larkin and Connolly. This was the only weapon which could have defeated the employers.

A letter from George Russell (AE) appeared in the *Irish Times* of October 7th, in which he bitterly condemned the greed of the employers. "Your insolence," he wrote, "and ignorance of the rights conceded to workers universally in the modern world were as incredible as your inhumanity. If you had between you a portion of soul as large as a threepenny bit, you would have sat night and day with the representatives of labour, trying this or that solution of the trouble, mindful of the women and children who at least were innocent of wrong against you. But no! you reminded labour you could always have your three square meals a day while it went hungry."[5]

In spite of Russell's attack and a government court of inquiry which found that the employers' document imposed "conditions which are contrary to individual liberty and which no workman or body of workmen could reasonably be expected to accept,"[6] the employers did not budge.

The lock-out continued through Christmas and into the New Year. In February with the people of Dublin starving and aid from Britain falling off, the workers began to return to work. In some cases the document was signed but in most cases it was not ever presented. Where it was signed it was disregarded. The lock-out was over; it was, as Connolly wrote, a drawn battle. The ITGWU was, of course, very weak, but it was still in existence. The employers had failed in their effort to crush the Dublin working class.

Connolly, summing up the lock-out in *The Irish Worker* of November 18th, 1914, wrote: "When that story is written (the whole epic story of 1913) by a man or woman with an honest heart and with a sympathetic insight into the travail of the poor, it will be a record of which Ireland may well be proud. It will tell of how the old women and young girls, long crushed and enslaved, dared to risk all, even life itself, in the struggle to make life more tolerable, more free of the grinding tyranny of the soulless Dublin employers. It will tell of how, like an inspiration there came to those Irish women and girls the thought that no free nation could be reared which tolerated the enslavement of its daughters to the worst forms of wage-slavery, and how in the glow of that inspiration they rose from their seats in the workshop or factory, and went out to suffer and struggle along with the men. It will tell of the general labourers, the men upon whose squalid tenements the sweet smelling flowers of capitalist culture derive their aroma, by whose horny hands and mangled bodies are brought the ease and safety of a class that hates and despises them, by whose ignorance their masters purchase their knowledge — it will tell how these labourers dared to straighten their bent backs, and looking in the faces of their rulers and employers, dared to express the will to be free. And it will tell how that spectacle of the slave of the underworld, looking his masters in the face without terror, and fearlessly proclaiming the kinship and unity of all with each and each with all, how that spectacle caught the imagination of all unselfish souls so that the skilled artisan took his place also in the place of conflict and danger, and the men and women of genius, the artistic and the literati, hastened to honour and serve those humble workers whom all had hitherto despised and scorned."[7]

The song *Dublin City*, (page 86), was written by Donagh MacDonagh, the son of Thomas MacDonagh the executed 1916 leader, to the tune *Preab san Ól*.

The violence used by employers through the police, provoked, naturally, an answering policy of violence from the workers. On August 26th 1913, during the lock-out, Larkin in a speech at Liberty Hall, declared: "If it is right and legal for the men of Ulster to arm, why would it not be right and legal for the men of Dublin to arm themselves to protect themselves."[8] In Wexford some time before this speech was made, when a worker had been killed in a police baton charge during a lock-out, the ITGWU official, P. T. Daly, had organised a workers' police force. It only lasted for the duration of the strike but in November 1913, with Larkin in jail, Connolly issued a manifesto which was posted up all over Dublin and appeared in *The Irish Worker:* "Fellow-workers, the employers are determined to starve you into submission, and if you resist, to club you, jail you, and kill you. We defy them! If they think they can carry on their industries without you, we will, in the words of the Ulster Orangemen, "Take steps to prevent it". It is our duty to find the ways and means. Be men now, or be for ever slaves."[9]

When Larkin was released from jail a victory meeting was called on November 13th at which Connolly said: "I am going to talk sedition. The next time we are out for a march I want to be accompanied by four battalions of trained men, with their corporals and sergeants. Why should we not drill and train men as they are doing in Ulster?"[10] Growing from the needs of the situation, the Citizen Army was soon organised and protected strikers at meetings and marches from the worst excesses of police violence. When the lock-out ended, however, members started leaving.

The playwright Sean O'Casey proposed that the army should be reorganised and a constitution adopted. This was done at a meeting in Liberty Hall on March 22nd 1914, when a committee was elected and the following constitution was adopted:

1. **That the first and last principle of the Irish Citizen Army** is the avowal that the ownership of Ireland, moral and material, is vested of right in the people of Ireland.
2. That the Irish Citizen Army shall stand for the absolute unity of Irish nationhood, and shall support the rights and liberties of the democracies of all nations.
3. That one of its objects shall be to sink all differences of birth, property and creed under the common name of the Irish people.
4. That the Citizen Army shall be open to all who accept the principle of equal rights and opportunities for the Irish people.
5. That before being enrolled, every applicant must, if eligible, be a member of his Trade's Union, such a Union to be recognised by the Irish Trades Union Congress.[11]

A new, smarter Citizen Army appeared in dark green uniforms and slouch hats. The few women members had equal rights with the men.

The army adopted as their symbol the now famous Starry Plough and before long a flag appeared bearing this emblem on a green background. Soon companies of this army were training and drilling at Clondalkin, Lucan, Swords, Finglas, Coolock, Kinsealy and Baldoyle, while the main body met at Croydon Park and Liberty Hall.

The army received some of the guns and ammunition successfully landed at Howth from Erskine Childers' yacht "Asgard". In a farewell message to the army in the *Irish Worker* of October 24th 1914, Larkin, who was leaving for America to raise funds for the ITGWU, wrote: "To my comrades of the Irish Citizen Army: in my absence Jim Connolly will take command. Bear yourselves before all men according to your past. Remember your constitution: on your oath — Ireland first, last, and all the time. Sobriety, unquestioned obedience, and keenes for drill be your motto."[12]

Connolly not only took over the leadership of the army, but the jobs of General Secretary of the ITGWU and Editor of the *Irish Worker*. Under his leadership the Citizen Army became more militant. With the outbreak of World War I and the conviction it brought to Connolly that a blow for Irish independence must be struck at this time of crisis, he and the army drew closer to advanced sections of the Irish Volunteers and the IRB.

In January 1916, the military committee of the Irish Republican Brotherhood had a meeting with Connolly lasting several days. A date for the Rising was decided and Connolly was co-opted onto the committee.

On the eve of the Rising, at the final mobilisation, Connolly addressed the Citizen Army and gave each man the opportunity to draw back. Not one availed of his offer. After the Rising the Citizen Army was reconstituted under Commandant James O'Neill. It was active against the Black and Tans during the War of Independence and on the Republican side during the Civil War until May 24th 1923 when the Republican 'cease fire' order brought the war and the Citizen Army to an end.

James Connolly and James Larkin, the founding fathers of the Irish labour movement, are figures of such importance not only nationally but internationally that any adequate account of their lives and works would extend far beyond the scope of this introduction. Connolly in particular, not only in his life but in his theoretical writing and journalism, laid the foundations on which might be built the workers' republic. From 1913 onwards Pearse was coming closer to socialist ideas, as can be seen by his later writings. The Proclamation of the Republic expresses the advanced thinking of Connolly, Pearse and some of the other leaders: "We declare the right of the people of Ireland to the ownership of Ireland, and to the unfettered control of Irish destinies, to be sovereign and indefeasible. The Republic guarantees religious and civil liberty, equal rights and equal opportunities to all its citizens, and declares its resolve to pursue the happiness and prosperity of the whole nation and of all its parts, cherishing all the children of the nation equally, and oblivious of the differences carefully fostered by an alien government, which have divided a minority from the majority in the past."[13]

That the realisation of this vision has been too long delayed is a reflection on the confusion and timidity of Connolly's successors, not on the validity of the vision itself.

The ballad on page 85 was written anonymously and sold on the streets of Dublin during Larkin's funeral in 1947.

Connolly himself wrote several songs and poems. The theme of *Be moderate*, (page 90), may have been suggested by *The Earth of All*, a poem by Gerald Massey, a member of the Christian Socialist Party of 1850.

Although in general Connolly's verse is less important and distinguished than his prose, *A Rebel Song*, (page 91), still sings well. It appeared first in 1903 in the May number of the Edinburgh paper *The Socialist*.

On the 12th of May 1916, Connolly, strapped to a chair in the yard of Kilmainham Jail, was executed by a firing squad. It was thought that because of the seriousness of his wounds he might be spared the fate of the other leaders, but characteristically William Martin Murphy's newspapaper, *The Independent*, implacably demanded his blood, declaring: "that no special leniency should be extended to some of the worst of the leaders whose cases have not yet been disposed of."[14] Connolly's death was an irreparable loss to the labour movement in Ireland.

"The son of a Welsh miner, a member of the firing squad that shot James Connolly, was so impressed by the bravery of the Great Leader that afterwards he paid a visit to Connolly's relatives to implore forgiveness. The following poem is an impression of the soldier's story to his comrades."[15] That is how the poet, Liam MacGabhann, introduces his poem, given here on page 94.

Notes

1. Donal Nevin *1913, Jim Larkin and the Dublin Lock-Out* p. 22.
2. Ibid p. 35.
3. Ibid p. 42.
4. Desmond Ryan (Ed.) *The Workers' Republic* p. 124.
5. Donal Nevin *Op. Cit.* p. 57.
6. Emmet Larkin *James Larkin: Irish Labour Leader 1876-1947* p. 122.
7. Desmond Ryan *Op. Cit.* pp. 171-172.
8. R. M. Fox *The History of the Citizen Army* p. 2.
9. C. Desmond Greaves *The Life and Times of James Connolly* p. 261.
10. Ibid p. 263.
11. R. M. Fox *Op. Cit.* p. 64.
12. Sean O'Casey *The Story of the Irish Citizen Army* p.225.
13. C. Desmond Greaves *Op. Cit.* p. 331.
14. *1916-1966 Easter Week Supplement to Irish Socialist* p. 5.
15. Liam MacGabhann *Rags, Robes and Rebels* p. 12.

THE STRUGGLE AGAINST FASCISM

The twenties and thirties of this century saw the growth and establishment in government of powerful fascist parties in various European countries — Italy, Spain and, most notoriously of all, Germany. Posing as defenders of the traditional values, cultural and religious, against the red menace of militant socialism that was developing in a Western Europe caught in throes of a capitalist crisis, and against the young USSR, gradually emerging as a formidable world power, the fascists were in reality a manifestation of the hysteria of the petty bourgeoisie, ready to throw in their lot with any political force prepared to guarantee them a social order stable enough to continue to give them shelter. Needless to say the strange posse of neurotic romantics, political adventurers, unemployed army officers and psychopaths found ready financial backing from the funds of capitalist corporations. In Germany the names of Krupps, Thyssen and Siemens deserve special mention as accomplices in the growth of Adolf Hitler's National Socialist (Nazi) Party.

Many communists and other socialists were imprisoned in Germany after the seizure of power by Adolf Hitler after the Reichstag fire of February 27th 1933. The song, *The Peat-Bog Soldiers*, (page 95), was written by an unnamed prisoner in the Borgermoor Camp near the Dutch Frontier. Its German name is "Die Moorsoldaten" and it first appeared in 1935 in a book of the same name, an account of 13 months' imprisonment in the camp, written by Wolfgang Langhoss. Since it was written the song has enjoyed a steady popularity amongst anti-fascists. A moving account is given by Fritz Selbmann (in *Neue Deutschland*, April 17th, 1965) of its power to strengthen the hearts of those in the clutches of a fascist dictatorship. He writes: "On the 3rd of September 1941, seventy prisoners lie in the bunks of a barrack room in a German concentration camp. They hear the shots outside, 465 on this particular night, and every shot kills a comrade, a brother, a communist. Every shot bores into their own hearts. They lie awake counting the shots, clenching their fists, trying not to cry out. Then something beautiful and terrible happens . . . in the farthest corner of the room a comrade begins to hum softly. The song is *The Peat-bog Soldiers*. Slowly, one by one, the others take up the tune and by the fourth line, seventy prisoners, all political, almost all communists, are singing this hymn of defiance."[1]

When the Popular Front was victorious in the Spanish Parliamentary elections in February 1936, immediately reactionary and fascist elements began plotting an uprising. This revolt, which began in July, was quickly put down by the government forces. Early in August, however, the fascist German and Italian governments lent their support to the army led by General Franco, the only considerable anti-government force, and transported 15,000 Spanish Troops, Foreign Legionnaires and Moroccans from Spanish Morocco where they were stationed to Jerez on the mainland of Spain. Thus began the Spanish Civil War, in which many young socialists and lovers of democracy from many lands fought and died to defend the Spanish Republic against the might of European fascism which was armed with the most modern and devastating weapons. Hitler made no secret of what he hoped would result from the war — the possession by the German armaments industry (Krupp) of Spain's raw materials. "We need a national government in Spain," he announced in 1937, "in order to protect the Spanish ore for ourselves."[2]

Volunteers from many countries — the Lincoln Brigade from the U.S.A., Garibaldi Brigade from Italy and the Connolly Column from Ireland — went to help the republican forces, but the French, British and American governments chose to ignore the open intervention of the fascist governments and allowed them to overthrow the constitutionally elected government of Spain. They were to pay dearly for this when the fascist alliance — the Axis powers — flushed with victory and in the pride of their new found strength turned on Britain and France with their now tried and tested weapons and tactics. 1939 marked the collapse of democracy in Spain, the establishment of General Franco as dictator and the opening of World War II in Europe.

3,350 Italian volunteers fought for the Spanish government, and 600 were killed in action. The song, *Bandiera Rossa*, (page 96), was in fact an Italian anti-fascist song written before the Spanish Civil War, but many volunteers from other countries brought it home with them from this war and it is sung today in many languages and in many parts of the world.

The International Brigade was formed of volunteers from 54 different nations — 2,000 from Britain of whom 500 were killed and 1,200 wounded, 132 from Ireland, 60 of whom died in action. The Irish volunteers were led by Frank Ryan and included men from the Communist Party of Ireland, the

Republican Congress, the IRA and other organisations. The young Irish poet, Charles Donnelly, and the British marxist philosopher, Christopher Caudwell, were among the many British and Irish who died at the battle of Jarama, celebrated in the song on page 97.

> "Death stalked the olive trees
> Picking his men
> His leaden finger beckoned
> Again and again"[3]

wrote John Lepper, a British volunteer in a poem describing the scene. The words spoken by Dolores Ibarruri, *La Pasionaria*, a communist member of Parliament, to the men of the International Brigade at its farewell parade in Barcelona in 1938, express something of the wild poetry and reckless idealism which characterised this tragic conflict:

"Mothers! Women! when the years pass by and the wounds of war are staunched; when the cloudy memory of the sorrowful bloody days returns in a present of freedom, love and wellbeing; when the feelings of rancour are dying away and when pride in a free country is felt equally by all Spaniards — then speak to your children. Tell them how, coming over seas and mountains, crossing frontiers bristling with bayonets, and watched for by ravening dogs thirsty to tear at their flesh, these men reached our country as crusaders for freedom. They gave up everything, their lovers, their country, home and fortune, fathers, mothers, wives, brothers, sisters and children and they came and told us: We are here. Your cause, Spain's cause, is ours. It is the cause of all advanced and progressive mankind.' Today they are going away. Many of them, thousands of them, are staying here with the Spanish earth for their shroud, and all Spaniards remember them with the deepest feeling.

"Comrades of the International Brigade! Political reasons, reasons of state, the welfare of that same cause for which you offered your blood with boundless generosity, are sending you back, some of you to your own countries and others to forced exile. You can go proudly. You are history. You are legend. You are the heroic example of democracy's solidarity and universality. We shall not forget you, and when the Olive Tree of peace puts forth its leaves again, mingled with the Laurels of the Spanish Republic's victory — come back!"[4]

Ewan MacColl used the same melody and opening verse of

a ballad telling of the death of a Scottish Militiaman in Spain in the war against Napoleon, for his poignant song about the death of a young Scottish shipyard worker in the Spanish Civil War, Jamie Foyers, (page 98).

Notes

1. Quoted in Diana Loeser *Ding Dong Dollar*, essay in *Essays in Honour of William Gallagher* p. 216.
2. Albert Norden *Thus Wars Are Made* p. 68.
3. Hugh Thomas *The Spanish Civil War* p. 489.
4. Ibid p.. 701-702.

THE TIMES THEY ARE A-CHANGIN'

In the decade following the end of World War II, there were as many profound social changes in the advanced industrial countries, and as great an awakening of a hunger for political and economic freedom in the colonial territories of the old empires as there had been after World War 1. The imperial powers in Europe which emerged from the war on the victorious side — Britain, France and Holland — had demonstrably less capacity for direct rule of their overseas possessions than before the war and were compelled by political and economic circumstances to grant independence — political, if not economic — to their subject peoples in Africa, Asia, Latin America and the Pacific.

Two great powers now dominated world politics — the USSR and the USA. Between the poles of these two forces, the world divided itself into two armed camps, producing a situation which bore a strong resemblance to warfare but without open military conflict — The Cold War. Within the Soviet Union and the United States this tension stimulated a fear of dissidence and non-conformity that manifested itself in the specially harsh repression of Stalin's last years and the ugly witch-hunts of socialists and liberals conducted by Senator Joseph McCarthy and the Un-American Activities Committee in the U.S.A.

Both these extremes produced reactions. Within the Soviet Union this was expressed in the person of Khruschev who, as General Secretary of the C.P.S.U., led an attack at the Twentieth Congress of the Party against the personality cult and policies of the deceased Stalin, and in the United States a more popular revulsion set in which expressed itself in many different ways. Chiefly it took the form of a general questioning of the values of the older generation and the policies of the American establishment by the youth of this, the most powerful and wealthy state in the world. The targets selected for attack by the youth and other pressure groups were diverse but they outlined a general and deeply-felt concern for a truly human way of life, more warm and spontaneous, less artificial and machine-conditioned, more caring and peaceful, less racist and family-centred. These feelings were echoed by the youth of the other advanced industrial nations and expressed themselves in agitation on such issues as Nuclear Disarmament, Civil Rights, the war in Vietnam, Environmental Pollution and so on.

The growth of militancy amongst the youth and sections of society with no previous tradition of organisation, coincided with a popular revival of interest in folk-song. Ewan MacColl and Peggy Seeger both as performers and composers did much to promote the cause of folk music. They made available hundreds of traditional songs and ballads to young people in their collections and records. In their own compositions they expressed the feelings of many thousands who shared their opinions on such scandals as nuclear weaponry and racial discrimination. Their songs *Brother won't you join in the line?* and *March with us today* were well known during the Campaign for Nuclear Disarmament. Of the many songs from that period it is Ian Campbell's *The Sun is Burning* which was most widely sung. I give it here on page 99.

At the great marches and rallies demanding full civil rights for black Americans, many songs defying the limits set on freedom of speech and movement were sung. The most famous is *We shall Overcome* which has become the anthem of protesters throughout the world, its words changing to suit the situation. Another song that grew from the Civil Rights Movement, describing some of the humiliating discrimination suffered by black Americans in their own country, is called *If you miss me at the back of the bus* and I give it on page 100.

The Un-American Activities Committee, a United States Senate sub-committee under the chairmanship of Senator Joseph McCarthy, caused much resentment among young people. Many sackings and purges occured as a result of its activities as people suffered for their opinions. *In contempt,* (page 101), was first published in the October 1950 issue of the American folk music magazine *Sing Out.*

In the sixties a young singer-composer emerged who seemed to embody the spirit of protest of that time. Bob Dylan captured so naturally, with his direct style of music and singing, the flavour of folk-song that Woody Guthrie, the foremost figure of the folk song movement, commented: "Pete Seeger's a singer of folk-songs, Jack Elliott's a singer of folk-songs but Bob Dylan's a folk-singer. Oh Christ! he's a folk singer all right!" His *The Times They are a-changin'*, (page 102), typifies the attitude of the young people who joined in the great crusades of that decade.

Towards the end of the sixties the issue of Civil Rights came to a head in Northern Ireland, where the Catholic population in that intensely sectarian statlet were beginning to chafe at their status as second class citizens.

In 1936 the British National Council on Civil Liberties had reported that the Special Powers Acts in Northern Ireland treated with contempt "The fundamental principles of democratic government" and that "Through the use of special powers individual liberty is no longer protected by law, but is at the arbitrary disposition of the executive. The abrogation of the rule of law has been so practised as to bring the freedom of the subject into contempt. The Northern Irish Government has used the Special Powers towards securing the domination of one particular faction and, at the same time, towards curtailing the lawful activities of its opponents. The driving of legitimate movements underground into illegality, the intimidating or branding as lawbreakers of their adherents, however innocent of crime, has tended to encourage violence and bigotry on the part of the government's supporters." It was against this background that the Northern Ireland Civil Rights Movement was born.

In February 1967, a Campaign for Social Justice in Northern Ireland was established in Dungannon. This lead to the establishment in the spring of 1968 of the Northern Ireland Civil Rights Association (NICRA). The first Civil Rights march was held successfully in Dungannon in August 1968. The events set out in the ballad *The 5th Day of October,* (page 103), occured when a Civil Rights march in Derry on October 5th 1968 was attacked by the police, using batons, water cannon and the dreaded CS gas. The Civil Rights movement went from strength to strength, winning many important concessions from Stormont. Before it was swamped by sectarian violence the campaign was a cause which could rally the support of all lovers of democracy there — Catholic and Protestant.

The policy of internment without trial introduced on August 9th 1971, during the premiership of Brian Faulkner, gave further substance to the trenchant words of Sydney Smith: "The moment the very name of Ireland is mentioned, the English seem to bid adieu to common feeling, common prudence and common sense, and to act with the barbarity of tyrants and the fatuity of idiots."[1]

It is hardly necessary to say it, but deprivation and poverty in Ireland are by no means the monopoly of the Northern Counties. There has been much harassment of travellers in recent times. The 1960 census of itinerants showed that of 1,198 families interviewed 931 of the fathers expressed a desire to remain living in one place. The census further showed that 12.5% of the travellers' children died before reaching the age of two. Of 6,904 children born alive, 859 died in the first two years. The 1963 report of the Commission on Itinerancy recommended the provision of serviced camping sites as the best means of ending itinerancy. In 1969. when one of these sites was built in Rahoon in Galway, local people forced nine travellers' families from the site which was then turned into a car-park. Their action gave birth to a new word in the English language, *Rahoonery* meaning the violent prejudice and hostility by the settled community against the settlement of travellers in their area. This shameful hostility still exists as recent events in Galway show. *The Travellers' Campaign,* (page 105), was written by a traveller named Joe Donohue and details their resistance to eviction from a makeshift school at Ballyfermot in the winter of 1963.

More and more people throughout the world find the apartheid policy of the South African government an offence against civilisation. Even those powers that have huge investments in the South African economy are being reluctantly compelled to consider action that might force the South African government to liberalise. Universal boycott of South African goods and an embargo on exports to, and investment in her would certainly be the most effective means that other nations could take to effect a rapid change, in spite of the hypocritical cant of that government that the black population would be the worst sufferers. Ewan Mac Coll wrote the powerful ballad on page 107 shortly after the Sharpville Massacre. On March 21st 1960, in the township of Sharpville, in the Transvaal, South Africa, police opened fire on a peaceful demonstration killing sixty-seven and wounding over a hundred-and-fifty people.

1. THE CUTTY WREN

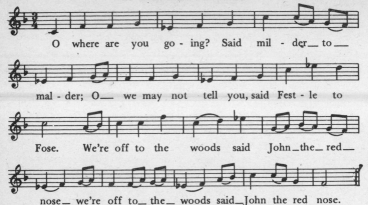

O where are you go-ing? Said mil-der— to— mal-der; O— we may not tell you, said Fest-le to Fose. We're off to the woods said John—the— red— nose— we're off to— the— woods said—John the red nose.

What will you do there said Milder to Malder
Oh we may not tell you said Festle to Fose
We'll shoot the Cutty Wren said John the Red Nose
We'll shoot the Cutty Wren said John the Red Nose.

How will you shoot her said Milder to Malder
Oh we may not tell you said Festle to Fose
With bows and arrows said John the Red Nose
With bows and arrows said John the Red Nose.

That will not do said Milder to Malder
Oh what will do then said Festle to Fose
Big guns and big cannons said John the Red Nose
Big guns and big cannons said John the Red Nose.

In what will you cook her said Milder to Malder
Oh we may not tell you said Festle to Fose
In pots and in pans said John the Red Nose
In pots and in pans said John the Red Nose.

Oh that will not do said Milder to Malder
Oh what will do then said Festle to Fose
Bloody bright brass cauldrons said John the Red Nose
Bloody bright brass cauldrons said John the Red Nose.

Who'll get the spare ribs said Milder to Malder
Oh we may not tell you said Festle to Fose
We'll give them all to the poor said John the Red Nose
We'll give them all to the poor said John the Red Nose.

Notes pp. 7-8.

2. THE ROCKS OF BAWN

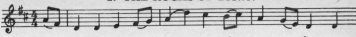

Come all you loy-al — he - roes wher - ev - er — that you

be, Don't hire with an - y — mas - ter till you know what you

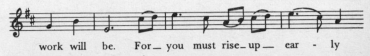

work will be. For — you must rise — up — ear - ly

from the clear day-light till dawn. I'm a-fraid you won't be —

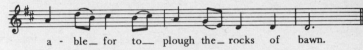

a - ble — for to — plough the — rocks of bawn.

My shoes they are well worn now and my stockings they
  are thin
My heart is always trembling afeared I might give in
My heart is nearly broken from the clear daylight till dawn
And I never will be able to plough the Rocks of Bawn.

My curse attend you Sweeney for you have me nearly robbed
You're sitting by the fireside with your feet upon the hob
You're sitting by the fireside from the clear daylight of dawn
But you never will be able to plough the Rocks of Bawn.

Oh rise up gallant Sweeney and give your horse some hay
And give him a good feed of oats before you go away
Don't feed him on soft turnips, put him out on your green
  lawn
And then he might be able to plough the Rocks of Bawn.

I wish the Queen of England would write to me in time
And place me in some regiment all in my youth and prime
I'd fight for Ireland's glory from the clear daylight till dawn
And I never would return again to plough the Rocks of Bawn.

Notes pp. 7-8.

3. SUCH A PARCEL OF ROGUES IN A NATION

Fare - weel to__ a' our Scot - tish__ fame Fare -
weel our an - cient glo - ry. Now__ Sark __ runs__
o'er the__ Sol - way__ sands and__ Tweed runs__ to the __
O - cean, To__ mark where Eng - land's Pro - vince stands;
Such a par - cel of rogues in a na - tion.

Fare - weel e - ven to the Scot - tish__ name Sae __
famed in mar - tial __ sto - ry.

What force or guile could not subdue
Thro' many warlike ages
Is wrought now by a coward few
For hireling traitors' wages.
The English steel we could disdain
Secure in valour's station
But English gold has been our bane
Such a parcel of rogues in a nation.

Oh would ere I had seen the day
That treason thus could sell us
My auld grey head had lain in clay
Wi Bruce and loyal Wallace.
But pith and power till my last hour
I'll make this declaration
We're bought and sold for English gold
Such a parcel of rogues in a nation.

Notes pp. 8-9.

4. WAE'S ME FOR PRINCE CHARLIE

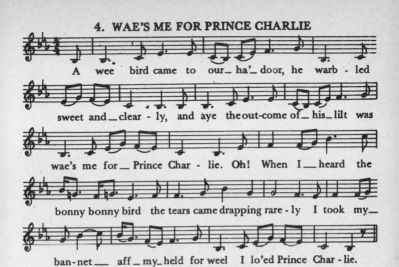

A wee bird came to our ha' door, he warb-led sweet and clear-ly, and aye the out-come of his lilt was wae's me for Prince Char-lie. Oh! When I heard the bonny bonny bird the tears came drapping rare-ly I took my ban-net aff my held for weel I lo'ed Prince Char-lie.

Said I, "My bird, my bonny bonny bird,
Is that a tale ye borrow?
Or is't some words ye've learnt by rote
Or a lilt o' dool and sorrow?"
"Oh! no, no, no!" the wee bird sang,
"I've flown sin' morning early;
But sic a day o' wind and rain!
Oh! wae's me for Prince Charlie!"

"On hills that are by right his ain,
He roams a lonely stranger;
On ilka hand he's press'd by want,
On ilka side by danger.
Yestreen I met him in a glen,
My heart near bursted fairly,
For sadly changed indeed was he
Oh! wae's me for Prince Charlie!"

"Dark night came on the tempest howl'd
Out-owre the hills and valleys;
And whare was't that your Prince lay doon
Whase hame should been a palace?
He row'd him in a highland plaid
Which cover'd him but sparely,
And slept beneath a bush o' broom
Oh! wae's me for Prince Charlie!"

Notes pp. 8-9.

5. LA MARSEILLAISE

Sol-diers of France the morn is break-ing the day of glo-ry dawns at last! See the ty-rant's ban-ner shak-ing as it base-ly streams in the blast. As it base-ly streams in the blast __ the field of bat-tle lies be-fore you fierce foe-men ad-vance in their pride, Con-fu-sion spread-ing far and wide while for aid your chil-dren im-plore you to arms __ and hence a-way __ To arms_this glo-rious day, March on march on brave sons of France to__ fame_ and vic-to-ry.

Ye tyrants quake, your day is over,
Detested now by friend and foe'
Who your base designs discover,
Ye shall die as traitors do,
Ye shall die as traitors do,
Each gallant heart with zeal o'erflowing
Goes eagerly forth at the call
Though some may for their country fall,
Others will hear bugles blowing.

Notes page 10.

6. HENRY JOY

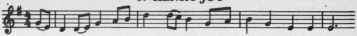

An Ul-ster man I am proud to be from the An-trim glens I come,

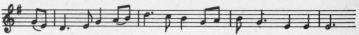

al-though I la-bour_ by the sea I have fol-lowed flag and drum.

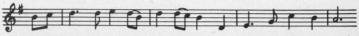

I have heard the mar-tial tramp of men; I've seen them fight and die.

Ah! Lads I well re-mem-ber when I _ fol-lowed Hen-ry Joy.

I pulled my boat up from the sea
I hid my sails away,
I hung my nets on a greenwood tree,
And I scanned the moonlit bay,
The Boys were out, and the Redcoats too;
I kissed my wife goodbye,
And in the shade of the greenwood glade,
Sure I followed Henry Joy.

In Antrim Town the tyrant stood,
He tore our ranks with ball,
But with a cheer and a pike to clear
We swept them o'er the wall.
Our pikes and sabres flashed that day
We won, but lost, ah! why?
No matter lads, I fought beside,
And shielded Henry Joy.

Ah! boys, for Ireland's cause we fought,
For her and home we bled,
Though pikes were few still our hearts beat true,
And five to one lay dead.
But many a lassie mourned her lad
And mother mourned her boy;
For youth was strong in that gallant throng,
Who followed Henry Joy.

(Continued overleaf)

In Belfast Town they built a tree,
And the Redcoats mustered there;
I watched them come as the beat of the drum,
Rolled out from the barrack square:
He kissed his sister and went aloft,
He bade a last goodbye;
My God! he died, sure I turned and cried,
"They have murdered Henry Joy!"

Notes pp. 11-12.

Continued from page 68

"For all you coal-owners great fortunes has made,
By those jovial men that works in the coal trade.
Now, how can you think for to prosper and thrive,
By wanting to starve your poor workmen alive?"

"Good woman," said he, "I must bid you farewell.
You give me a dismal account about hell.
If this be all true that you say unto me,
I'll go home and with my poor men I'll agree."

So all you gay gentlemen with riches in store,
Take my advice and be good to the poor,
And if you do this, all things will gang well,
And perhaps it will save you from going to hell.

So come ye poor pitmen and join heart and hand,
For when you're off work, all trade's at a stand,
In the town of Newcastle all cry out amain:
"Oh, gin the pits were at work once again."

Well, the pit gates are locked, little more I've to say,
I was turned out of my house on the thirteenth of May.
But it's now to conclude and I'll finish my song,
I hope you'll relieve me and let me carry on.

Notes page 24.

Continued from page 60

For a' that an' a' that
Their dignities an' a' that
The pith o' sense an' pride o' worth
Are higher rank that a' that.

Than let us pray that come it may
As come it will for a' that
That sense and worth o'er a' the earth
Shall bear the gree an' a' that
For a' that an' a' that
It's coming yet for a' that
That man to man the world o'er
Shall brothers be for a' that

Notes pp. 12-13.

Continued from page 61

Oh well I do remember the year of '48
When I rose with comrades brave and true to battle against
fate.
I was hunted through the hills by slaves who served a foreign
Queen
And that's another reason why I left old Skibbereen.

Oh father dear, the day will come when vengeance loud will
call
When Irish men with faces stern will rally one and all.
I'll be the man to lead the van beneath our flag of green
And loud and high we'll raise the cry — Revenge for Skibber-
een

Notes pp. 15-16.

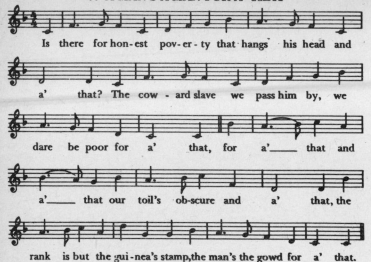

Is there for hon-est pov-er-ty that hangs his head and
a' that? The cow-ard slave we pass him by, we
dare be poor for a' that, for a'___ that and
a'___ that our toil's ob-scure and a' that, the
rank is but the gui-nea's stamp, the man's the gowd for a' that.

What though on hamely fare we dine
Wear hoddin grey an' a' that
Gie fools their silks and knaves their wine
A man's a man for a' that
For a' that an' a' that
Their tinsel show an' a' that
The honest man tho' 'e'er sae poor
Is king o' men for a' that.

Ye see yon birkie ca'd a lord
Wha struts an' stares an' a' that
Tho' hundreds worship at his word
He's but a coof for a' that
For a' that an' a' that
His ribband star an' a' that
The man o' independent mind
He looks an' laughs at a' that.

A prince can mak' a belted knight
A marquis duke an' a' that
But an honest man's aboon his might
Gude faith he mauna fa' that

Continued on previous page

60

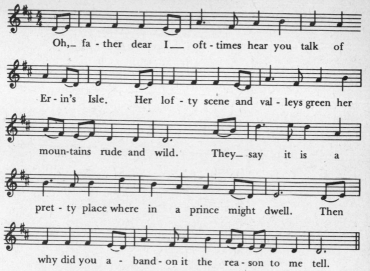

Oh,— fa - ther dear I— oft - times hear you talk of
Er - in's Isle. Her lof - ty scene and val - leys green her
moun-tains rude and wild. They— say it is a
pret - ty place where in a prince might dwell. Then
why did you a - band - on it the rea - son to me tell.

My son I loved my native land with energy and pride
'Till a blight came over all the land — my sheep and cattle
    died.
My rent and taxes were too high and them I couldn't redeem
And that's the cruel reason why I left old Skibbereen.

Oh well I do remember that bleak December day
The landlord and the sheriff came to drive us all away
They set my roof on fire with their demon yellow spleen
And that's another reason why I left old Skibbereen.

Your mother too, God rest her soul, fell on the snowy ground
She fainted in her anguish, seeing the desolation round.
She never rose, but passed away from life to mortal dream
And that's another reason why I left old Skibbereen.

Ah you were only two years old and feeble was your frame
I could not leave you with my friends — you bore your
    father's name.
I wrapped you in my cóta mór at the dead of night unseen
And heaved a sigh and bade goodbye to dear old Skibbereen.

Continued on page 59.

9. THE WEST'S ASLEEP

While ev-'ry side a vi - gil keep the West's a-sleep the
O long and well may Er - in weep when Conn-acht lies in

West's a-sleep.
slum-ber deep. There lake and plain smile fair and free and

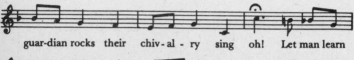

guar-dian rocks their chiv - al - ry sing oh! Let man learn

lib - er - ty from slash - ing wind and lash - ing sea.

That chainless wave and lovely land
Freedom and nationhood demand.
Be sure the great God never planned
For slumbering slaves a home so grand,
And long a brave and haughty race
Honoured and sentinelled the place
Sing Oh! not even their sons' disgrace
Can quite destroy their glory's trace.

For often in O'Connor's van
To triumph dashed each Connacht clan
And fleet as deer the Normans ran
Through Corrshliabh Pass and Ard Ratháin.
And later times saw deeds as brave
And glory guards Clanricard's grave
Sing Oh! they died their land to save
At Aughrim's slopes and Shannon's wave.

And if when all a vigil keep
The West's asleep the West's asleep,
Alas! and well my Erin weep
That Connacht lies in slumber deep.
But Hark! some voice like thunder spake
The West's awake, the West's awake!
Sing, oh hurray! let England quake!
We'll watch till death for Erin's sake.
Notes pp. 15-16.

10. SONG OF THE LOWER CLASSES

Words: Ernest Jones
Tune: "My old friend John".

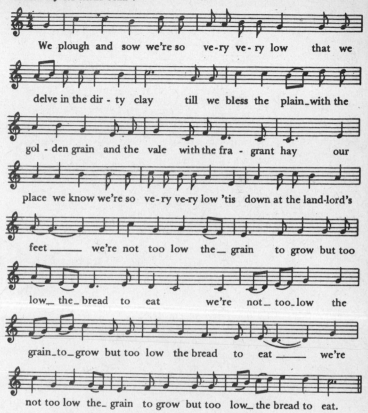

We plough and sow we're so ve-ry ve-ry low that we delve in the dir-ty clay till we bless the plain with the gol-den grain and the vale with the fra-grant hay our place we know we're so ve-ry ve-ry low 'tis down at the land-lord's feet we're not too low the grain to grow but too low the bread to eat we're not too low the grain to grow but too low the bread to eat we're not too low the grain to grow but too low the bread to eat.

Down, down we go, we're so very, very low
To the hell of the deep sunk mines
But we gather the proudest gems that glow
When the crown of the despot shines.
And when e'er he lacks upon our backs
Fresh loads he deigns to lay
We're far too low to vote the tax
But not too low to pay.

Continued on page 65

11. THE INTERNATIONALE

A-rise ye starvlings from your slum-bers, A-rise ye crim-i-nals of

want, for rea - son in re-volt now thun-ders and at last ends the

age of cant. Now a - way with all su-per-sti - tions ser-vile

mass - es a-rise! A - rise we'll change forth-with the old con -

Chorus

di - tions and spurn the dust to win the prize. Then ___

com-rades come ral - ly and the last fight let us face. The

In - ter - na - tion - al _____ U-nites the hu-man race

Then com-rades come ral - ly and the last fight let us

face The In - ter - na - tion-al U-nites the hu-man race.

No saviours from on high deliver
No trust have we in prince or peer
Our own right hand the chains must shiver
Chains of hatred, of greed and fear
Ere the thieves will disgorge their booty
And to all give a happier lot
Each at his forge must do his duty
And strike the iron while it's hot.
Chorus

We peasants, artisans and others
Enrolled among the sons of toil
Let's claim the earth henceforth for brothers
Drive the indolent from the soil.
On our flesh too long has fed the raven
We've too long been the vulture's prey
But now farewell the spirit craven
The dawn brings in a brighter day.
Chorus

Notes page 21.

Continued from page 63

We're low, we're low, we're very, very low
And yet from our fingers glide
The silken flow and the robes they glow
Round the limbs of the sons of pride.
And what we get, and what we give
We know and we know our share
We're not too low the cloth to weave
But too low the cloth to wear.

We're low, we're low, we're very, very low
And yet when the trumpets ring
The thrust of a poor man's arm will go
Through the heart of the proudest king.
We're low, we're low, mere rabble we know
We're only the rank and file
We're not too low to kill the foe
But too low to share the spoil.

Notes pp. 17-18.

12. THE RED FLAG

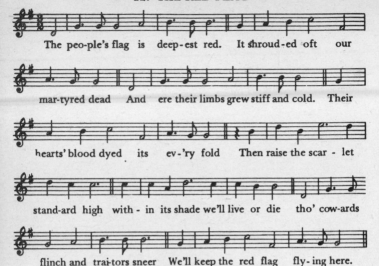

The peo-ple's flag is deep-est red. It shroud-ed oft our
mar-tyred dead And ere their limbs grew stiff and cold. Their
hearts' blood dyed its ev-'ry fold Then raise the scar - let
stand-ard high with - in its shade we'll live or die tho' cow-ards
flinch and trai-tors sneer We'll keep the red flag fly-ing here.

Look round, the Frenchman loves his blaze
The sturdy German chants his praise
In Moscow's vaults its hymns were sung
Chicago swells the surging song.

It waved above our infant might
When all ahead seemed dark as night
It witnessed many a deed and vow
We must not change its colour now.

It well recalls the triumphs past
It gives the hope of peace at last
The banner bright — the symbol plain
Of human right and human gain.

It suits to-day the weak and base
Whose minds are fixed on self and place
To cringe before the rich man's frown
And have the sacred emblem down.

With heads uncovered swear we all
To bear it onward till we fall
Come dungeons dark or gallows grim
This song shall be our parting hymn.   *Notes page 21-22.*

13. THE COAL-OWNER AND THE PITMAN'S WIFE

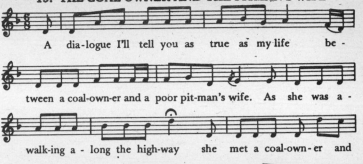

A dia-logue I'll tell you as true as my life between a coal-own-er and a poor pit-man's wife. As she was a-
walk-ing a-long the high-way she met a coal-own-er and
this she did say, der-ry down, down down der-ry down.

"Good morning, Lord Firedamp," this woman she said,
"I'll do you no harm sir, so don't be afraid.
If you'd been where I've been the most of my life,
You wouldn't turn pale at a poor pitman's wife."

"Then where do you come from?" the owner he cries,
"I come from hell," the poor woman replies.
"If you come from hell then come tell me right plain,
How you contrived to get out again."

"Aye, the way I got out, the truth I will tell,
They're turning the poor folk all out of hell.
This is to make room for the rich wicked race,
For there is a great number of them in that place.

"And the coal-owner is the next on command,
To arrive in hell, as I understand,
For I heard the old devil say as I came out:
"The coal-owners all had received their rout".

"Then how does the old devil behave in that place?"
"Oh sir, he is cruel to that rich wicked race.
He is far more crueller that you can suppose,
Even like a mad bull with a ring through his nose."

"If you be a coal-owner, sir, take my advice,
Agree with your men and give then a full price,
For if and you do not, I know very well,
You'll be in great danger of going to hell."

Continued on page 58

67

14. THE DURHAM LOCK-OUT

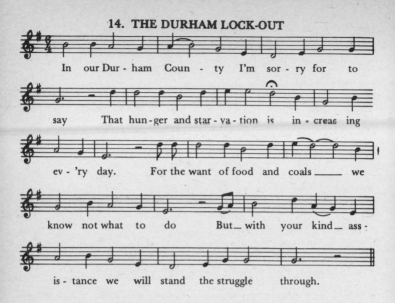

In our Dur-ham Coun-ty I'm sor-ry for to say That hun-ger and star-va-tion is in-creas-ing ev-'ry day. For the want of food and coals ___ we know not what to do But ___ with your kind ___ ass-is-tance we will stand the struggle through.

In our Durham county I am sorry to say
That hunger and starvation is increasing every day,
For the want of food and coals, we know not what to do,
But with your kind assistance we will stand the struggle through.

I need not state the reason why we have been brought so low
The masters have behaved unkind, which everyone will know,
Because we won't lie down and let them treat us as they like,
To punish us, they've stopped the pits and caused the present
    strike.

The pulley wheels have ceased to move which went so swift
    around,
The horses and the ponies too all brought from underground,
Our work is taken from us now, they care not if we die,
For they can eat the best of food, and drink the best when dry.

The miner and his wife too, each morning have to roam,
To seek for bread to feed the hungry little ones at home.
The flour barrel is empty now, their true and faithful friend,
Which makes the thousands wish today the strike was at an
    end.

We have done our very best as honest working men,
To let the pits commence again, we've offered to them ten,
The offer they will not accept, they firmly do demand,
Thirteen and a half per cent, or let the collieries stand.

Let them stand or let them lie or do with them as they choose,
To give them thirteen and a half we ever shall refuse.
They're always willing to receive, but not inclined to give,
Very soon they won't allow a working man to live.

With tyranny and capital they never seem content,
Unless they are endeavouring to take from us per cent.
If it was due, what they request, we willingly would grant.
We know it's not, therefore, we cannot give them what they
    want.

The miners of Northumberland we shall for ever praise,
For being so kind in helping us these tyrannising days.
We thank the other counties too, that have been doing the
    same,
For every man who hears this song will know we're not to
    blame.

Notes page 25.

Continued from page 70

But cheer up there's good friends that support us
Aye an' England depends on us a'
An' we'll prove that we're true to the movement
An' victory shall let the world know
That Tynesiders will never be conquered
By masters that care not for them
And if masters is meant to be masters
Let them find there's men meant to be men.

Notes page 26.

15. THE STRIKE

Come me can-ny Tyne-si-ders and lis-ten to a
song that I'm cer-tain you'll like and I'll whis-per a word
kind and chee-ring to the man-y poor fel-lows on strike.
Let them keep up their hearts as they have done. There's a
day for the true and the brave, and the time would come
yet when the mas-ters will find out a me-chan-ic's no slave.

Is nine hours an' unreasonable movement?
Is't not plenty to labour for men?
Let them that condemn'd have a try on it
And see if they'll alter such plan
An' if long hours industry increases
Have they found out with the hours they 've tried
Their capital grows through our labour
Why it's more to their shame that they'll find.

But a day will soon come when they'll welcome
The old hands they've so often employed
Then the foreigners' strength will be shaken
From licence that they've long enjoyed
In makin' therselves their own masters
An' workin' just when they'd a mind
If the masters pretend to be blind to it
Why it's more to their shame that they'll find.

Continued on page 69

16. FOURPENCE A DAY

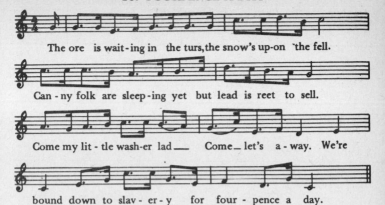

The ore is wait-ing in the turs, the snow's up-on the fell.

Can-ny folk are sleep-ing yet but lead is reet to sell.

Come my lit-tle wash-er lad — Come — let's a-way. We're

bound down to slav-er-y for four-pence a day.

It's early in the morning we rise at five o'clock,
And the little slaves come to the door to knock, knock, knock.
Come, my little washer lad, come let's away.
It's very hard to work for fourpence a day.

My Father was a miner and lived down in the town,
Twas hard work and poverty that always kept him down.
He aimed for me to go to school, but brass he couldn't pay,
So I had to go to the washing rake for fourpence a day.

My Mother rises out of bed with tears on her cheeks,
Puts my wallet on my shoulders which has to serve a week.
It often fills her great big heart when she unto me does say:
"I never thought thou would have worked for fourpence a
day."

Fourpence a day, my lad, and very hard the work,
And never a pleasant look from a gruffy-looking turk.
His conscience it may fail and his heart it may give way,
Then he'll raise us our wages to ninepence a day.

Notes pp. 26-27.

17. THE BANKS OF THE DEE

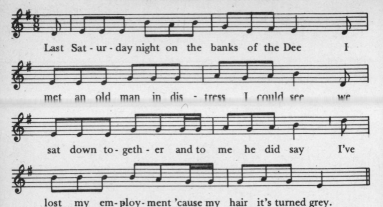

Last Sat-ur-day night on the banks of the Dee I met an old man in dis-tress I could see we sat down to-geth-er and to me he did say I've lost my em-ploy-ment 'cause my hair it's turned grey.

Chorus

I am an old miner, aged fifty and six
If I could get lots, I would raffle me picks
I'd raffle them, I'd sell 'em, I'd throw them away
For I can't get employment, me hair it's turned grey.

When I was a young chap I was just like the rest
Each day in the pit I'd do my very best
When I had a loose place I'd be filling all day
Not a fifty and six, me hair it's turned grey.

Last Wednesday night to the reckoning I went
To the colliery office I went straight fornenst*
I'd just got me paypacket, I was walking away
When they gave me me notice, 'cause me hair it's turned grey.

Now all you young fellows it's you that's to blame
If you get good places you'll do just the same
If you get good places you'll hew them away
But you're bound to regret it when your hair it's turned grey.

"straight fornenst" means "just opposite."

Notes page 27.

18. WILLIAM BROWN

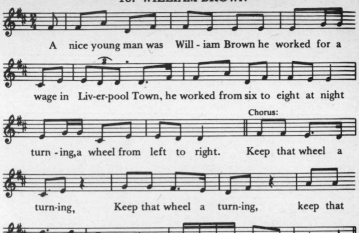

A nice young man was Will-iam Brown he worked for a
wage in Liv-er-pool Town, he worked from six to eight at night
turn-ing, a wheel from left to right. *Chorus:* Keep that wheel a
turn-ing, Keep that wheel a turn-ing, keep that
wheel a turn-ing and do a lit-tle more each day. —

The boss one day to William came
Saying look here young what's-your-name
We're not content with what you do
Work a little harder or its out with you. *Chorus*

So William turned and he made her run
Three times round in the time of one
He turned so fast he soon was made
The Lord high turner of his trade. *Chorus*

William turned with the same sweet smile
And all the goods grew to such a pile
They filled the room and the room next door
And overflowed to the basement floor. *Chorus*

When the nation heard of his wondrous tale
His picture appeared in the Sketch and the Mail
The railways ran excursions down
All to look at William Brown. *Chorus*

But sad the sequel is to tell
He turned out more than his boss could sell
The market slumped and the price went down
Seven more days and they sacked young Brown. *Chorus*

Notes page 27.

73

19. MY MASTER AND I

Says the mas-ter to me, is it true what I'm told, your
name on the books of the Un-ion's en-rolled. I can nev-er allow that a work-man of mine with wick-ed dis-turb-ers of the
peace should com-bine. I give you fair warn-ing mind
what you're a-bout, I shall put my foot on it and
tram-ple it out, which side your bread's but-tered I'm
sure you can see so de-cide now at once for the Un-ion or me.

I will give you fair warning mind what you're about
I shall put my foot on it and trample it out
Which side your bread's buttered I'm sure you can see
So decide now at once for the union or me.

Says I to my master it's perfectly true
That I'm in the union and I'll stick to it too
And if between union and you I must choose
I've plenty to win and I've little to lose.

For twenty years mostly my bread has been dry
So to butter it now I shall certainly try
And though I respect you remember I'm free
No master in England shall trample on me.

Says the master to me just a word or two more
We never have quarrelled on matters before
If you stick to the union 'ere long I'll be bound
You'll come and ask me for more wages all round.

Now I can't afford more than two bob a day
When I look at the rent and the taxes I pay
And the crops are so injured by game as you see
If it's hard for you then it's hard for me.

Says I to the master I do not see how
Any need has arisen for quarrelling now
And though likely enough we shall ask for more wage
I promise you we shan't get first in a rage.

Here comes Mr. Taylor so stout and so bold
The head of the labourers' union I'm told
He's persuaded the men to stick up for their rights
And they say he's been giving the farmers the gripes.

Notes pp. 27-28.

20. SOLIDARITY FOREVER

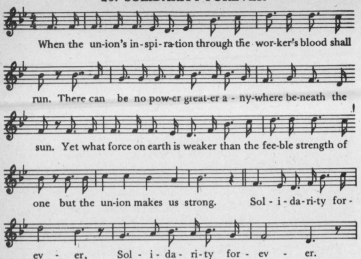

When the un-ion's in-spi-ra-tion through the wor-ker's blood shall run. There can be no pow-er great-er a-ny-where be-neath the sun. Yet what force on earth is weaker than the fee-ble strength of one but the un-ion makes us strong. Sol-i-da-ri-ty for-ev-er, Sol-i-da-ri-ty for-ev-er. Sol-i-da-ri-ty for-ev-er, For the un-ion makes us strong.

They have taken untold millions that they never toiled to earn
But without our brain and muscle not a single wheel would turn
We can break their haughty power, earn our freedom when we learn
That the union makes us strong.

It is we who ploughed the prairies, built the cities where they trade
Dug the mines and built the workshops, endless miles of railroad laid
Now we stand outcast and starving midst the wonders we have made
But the union makes us strong.

In our hands is placed a power greater than their hoarded gold
Greater than their armies magnified a thousand fold
We can bring to birth a new world from the ashes of the old
For the union makes us strong.

Notes pp. 29-30.

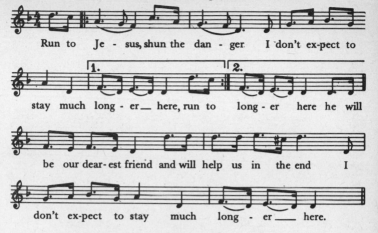

Oh, I thought I heard them say,
There were lions in the way.
I don't expect to stay much longer here.

Chorus

Many mansions there will be,
One for you and one for me.
I don't expect to stay much longer here.

Chorus

Notes page 32.

22. THE LUDLOW MASSACRE

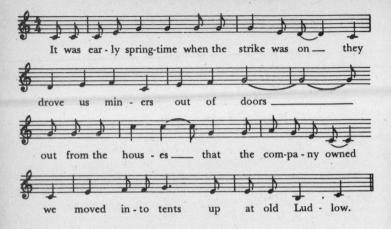

It was ear-ly spring-time when the strike was on — they drove us min-ers out of doors _____ out from the hous-es _____ that the com-pa-ny owned we moved in-to tents up at old Lud-low.

I was worried bad about the children,
Soldiers guarding the railroad bridge,
Every once in a while the bullets would fly,
Kick up gravel under my feet.

We were so afraid you would kill our children,
We dug us a cave that was seven foot deep,
Carried our young ones and a pregnant women,
Down inside the cave to sleep.

That very night your soldiers waited,
Until us miners was asleep,
You snuck around our little tent town,
Soaked our tents with kerosene.

You struck a match and the blaze it started,
You pulled the triggers of your gatling guns,
I made a run for the children but the fire wall stopped me,
Thirteen children died from you guns.

I carried my blanket to a wire fence corner,
Watched the fire till the blaze died down,
I helped some people grab their belongings,
While your bullets killed us all around.

I never will forget the look on the faces
Of the men and women that awful day,
When we stood around to preach their funerals
And lay the corpses of the dead away.

We told the Colorado Governor to phone the President,
Tell him to call off his National Guard,
But the National Guard belonged to the Governor,
So he didn't try so very hard.

Our women from Trinidad they hauled some potatoes,
Up to Walsenburg in a little cart,
They sold their potatoes and brought some guns back,
And they put a gun in every hand.

The state soldiers jumped us in the wire fence corner,
They did not know that we had these guns,
And the red-neck miners mowed down these troopers.
You should have seen those poor boys run.

We took some cement and walled the cave up,
Where you killed these thirteen children inside,
I said: "God bless the mine workers' union."
And then I hung my head and cried.

Notes pp. 30-31.

23. OH! FREEDOM

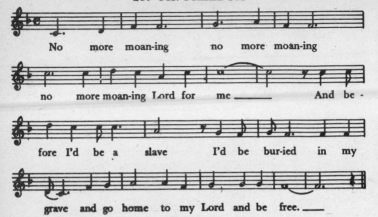

No more moan-ing no more moan-ing no more moan-ing Lord for me ____ And be-fore I'd be a slave I'd be bur-ied in my grave and go home to my Lord and be free. ____

No more mourning, no more mourning,
No more mourning over me, over me
And before I'll be a slave
I'll be buried in my grave
And go home to my Lord and be free

No more weeping, no more weeping,
No more weeping over me, over me
And before I'll be a slave
I'll be buried in my grave
And go home to my Lord and be free

Oh! what singing, Oh! what singing
Oh! what singing over me, over me
And before I'll be a slave
I'll be buried in my grave
And go home to my Lord and be free

Oh! what shouting, Oh! what shouting
Oh! what shouting over me, over me
And before I'll be a slave
I'll be buried in my grave
And go home to my Lord and be free

Oh! Oh! freedom, Oh! Oh! freedom
Oh! Oh! freedom over me, over me
And before I'll be a slave
I'll be buried in my grave
And go home to my Lord and be free

Notes pp. 29-32

24. MY WILL

My will is easy to decide
For there is nothing to divide
My kin don't need to fuss and moan
"Moss does not cling to rolling stones."

My body? — Oh! — If I could choose
I would to ashes it reduce
And let the merry breezes blow
My dust to where some flowers grow.

Perhaps some fading flower then
Would come to life and bloom again.
This is my last and final will.
Good luck to all of you,
                                    Joe Hill.

The work-ers on the S. P. line to strike sent out a call; But Ca - sey Jones the en - gi-neer he would-n't strike at all; His boil- er it was leak-ing and its driv-ers on the bum and his en-gine and its bear- ings they were all out of plumb.

Chorus:

Ca-sey Jones kept his junk pile run-ning, Ca-sey Jones was work-ing dou-ble time, Ca-sey Jones got a wood-en med-al for be - ing good and faith-ful on the S. P. line.

The workers said to Casey:
"Won't you help us win this strike"
But Casey said "let me alone.
You'd better take a hike."
Then Casey's wheezy engine
Ran right off
the worn-out track
With an awful crack.

Casey Jones, hit the river bottom
Casey Jones, broke his blooming spine
Casey Jones, became an Angeleno
He took a trip to Heaven on the S.P. line.

When Casey Jones got up to Heaven
To the pearly gate
He said "I'm Casey Jones
The guy that pulled the S.P. freight"
"You're just the man" said Peter
"Our musicians are on strike
You can get a job a-scabbing
Anytime you like"

Casey Jones, got a job in Heaven
Casey Jones, was doing might fine
Casey Jones, went scabbing on the angels
Just like he did to workers on the S.P. line

The Angels got together
And they said it wasn't fair
For Casey Jones to go around
A-scabbing everywhere
The angels' union no 23
They sure were there
And they promptly fired Casey
Down the Golden Stair.

Casey Jones went to hell a-flying
"Casey Jones," the devil said, "Oh Fine!
Casey Jones, get busy shoveling sulphur
That's what you get for scabbing on the S.P. line."

Notes pp. 36.

I dreamed I saw Joe Hill last night a-live as you and me. _____ Says I "But Joe you're ten years dead" "I nev-er died" says he _____ "I nev-er died" says he "I nev-er died" says he.

"In Salt Lake City," Joe says I,
Him standing by my bed,
"They framed you on a murder charge"
Says Joe: "I've not been dead"
Says Joe: "I've not been dead"

"The copper bosses killed you, Joe"
"They shot you, Joe" says I.
"Takes more than guns to kill a man,"
Says Joe, "I didn't die"
Says Joe, "I didn't die"

And there was Joe as big as life
And smiling with his eyes
Says Joe: "What they could never kill
Went on to organise."
"Went on to organise."

From San Diego up to Maine
In every mine and mill
Where workers strike and organise
It's there you'll find Joe Hill
It's there you'll find Joe Hill

I dreamed I saw Joe Hill last night
Alive as you and me
Says I: "But Joe you're ten years dead"
"I never died" says he
"I never died" says he.

Notes page 36.

27. JIM LARKIN RIP

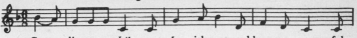

Come lis-ten a-while you Ir-ish-men and hear my mourn-ful

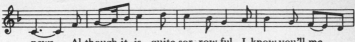

news— Al-though it is quite sor-row-ful I know you'll me—

cuse— come join my lam-en-ta - tion for one who was— our

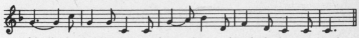

friend— he led the tor-tured wor-kers and made the boss-es bend.

A great man like Jim Larkin, we never can replace.
He fought our fight in dark '13 when the peelers he did face.
We lost our fight, but still we won, for Jim was not undone
And as the troubled years rolled on, his fight and ours he won.

When Ireland honours heroes bold, who fought to make her
free
The name of brave Jim Larkin will be there for all to see.
He fought to save the working man from bondage and from
woe,
And his name will long be honoured, no matter where you go.

He was treated to the batons by the forces of the crown
But bullies' guns or batons they could never keep him down.
The worker is a freeman now, by his persevering fight,
And his prospects for the future have never been so bright.

So, God rest your soul, Jim Larkin, may heaven be your home.
May St. Patrick take you to the land from where you'll never
roam.
And when a day in Ireland dawns that north and south are
free,
We will think of one great fighting man and just say: R.I.P.

Notes page 42.

28. DUBLIN CITY

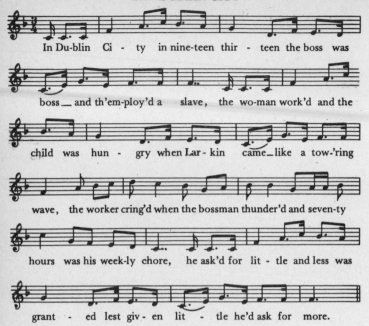

In Dublin City in nineteen thirteen the boss was boss— and th'employ'd a slave, the woman work'd and the child was hungry when Larkin came— like a tow'ring wave, the worker cring'd when the bossman thunder'd and seventy hours was his weekly chore, he ask'd for little and less was granted lest given little he'd ask for more.

Then along came Larkin, so dark and handsome,
A powerful man with a mighty tongue,
The voice of Labour, the voice of Justice
And he was gifted and he was young.
Then on came Larkin to Nineteen Thirteen,
A powerful man with a mighty tongue,
He raised the worker, he gave him courage,
He was the leader and the workers sung.

In the month of August the bossman told us
No union man for him would work.
We stood by Larkin. We told the boss man
To fight, to starve we would not shirk.
Eight months we fought and eight months we starved,
We followed Larkin through thick and thin,
But foodless homes and crying children
They broke our hearts and we could not win.

When Larkin left us we seemed defeated.
The sky seemed dark for our workless men.
But Connolly rose with new hope and counsel.
He gave the slogan: "We'll rise again."
In Dublin City in Nineteen Sixteen
The British Army they burned the town.
They shelled the city, they took the leaders.
The harp was shattered beneath the crown.

The shot MacDonagh and Pearse and Plunkett.
They shot MacDermott and Clarke and brave.
From bleak Kilmainham they took Ceannt's body
To Arbour Hill to a quicklime grave.
But last of all the seven captains,
A dying man, they shot Connolly,
The Labour leader, the voice of freedom,
Who gave his life that men might be free.

Notes pp. 37-40.

THE CITIZEN ARMY

The Citizen Army is out today and if you wonder why
Go ask the lords of the tram-lined way if their cash returns
be high.
'Tisn't the bosses who bear the brunt, 'tisn't you and I,
But the women and kids whose tears are hid as the strikers go
stumbling by.
The docker loads two hundred tons in his master's ship per day.
At night the docker's daughter bends her weary limbs to pray.
From the old North Wall to Liberty Hall was a deadline of
unskilled.
They heaved and hauled when the bosses called and stopped
when the bosses willed.

The Citizen Army is out today and if you wonder why
Go ask the troops in the masters' pay if the blood on their
guns be dry.
Ah, well, they won and the baton and gun have swung where
the dead men lie.
For the women and kids whose tears are hid as the wounded
go stumbling by.
Jim Connolly watches ships go out through flags at Kingstown
Pier
And starving Dublin sends its toll of guard and fusilier
Food for the guns that over the world have thundered murder's
peace
And Dublin's broken union men die first on Flanders' fields.

The Citizen Army is out today and if you wonder why
Jim Larkin came this way to nail the bosses' lie.
That the iron gyves on their limbs and lives would crush them
till they die!
Those women and kids whose tears are hid as the strikers go
marching by.
The docker and carter and heaver of coal, were only the back-
wash then
Till Larkin built the union up and the bosses feared again.
From the old North Wall to Liberty Hall came that deadline
of unskilled
In a new-born fight for the workers' rights that the bosses
thought they had killed.

The Citizen Army is out today and if you wonder why
Go ask the men in the grey and green why the Plough and
Stars flag flies.
Tisn't only the bosses we challenge now, 'tis Connolly has
cast the die,
For the women and kids whose tears are hid as the soldiers
go marching by.
Four hundred bosses planned to break that deadline of un-
skilled,
Four hundred bosses drink tonight for Connolly is killed.
But dead or alive, there are those who strive a glorious thing
to do,
For Connolly built that union up, for the likes of me and you.

The Citizen Army is out today and if you wonder why
Go ask the lords of the banking house if their cash returns be
high.
For they are there and we are here, and a fight to the knife
again.
The Citizen Army is out today; come workers, are ye men?

Notes pp. 39-43.

30. BE MODERATE

Some men faint hearted ever seek
Our programme to retouch
And will insist when e'er they speak
That we demand too much
'Tis passing strange yet I declare
Such statements cause me mirth
For our demands most modest are
We only want The Earth.

Be moderate the trimmers cry
Who dread the tyrants' thunder
You ask too much and people fly
From you aghast in wonder
'Tis passing strange for I declare
Such statements give me mirth
For our demands most modest are
We only want the The Earth.

Our masters all a godly crew
Whose hearts throb for the poor
Their sympathies assure us too
If our demands were fewer
Most generous souls; but please observe
What they enjoy from birth
Is all we ever had the nerve
To ask. that is The Earth.

The labour fakir full of guile
Base doctrine ever preaches
And while he bleeds the rank and file
Tame moderation teaches
Yet in his despite we'll see the day
When with sword in its girth
Labour shall march in war array
To seize its own, The Earth.

For labour long with sighs and tears
To its oppressors knelt
But never yet to aught save fears
Did heart of tyrant melt
We need not kneel, our cause is high
Of true men there's no dearth
And our victorious rallying cry
Shall be "We Want The Earth!" *Notes page 42.*

31. A REBEL SONG

Come work-ers sing a re-bel song, a song of love and hate, of love un-to the low-ly and of ha-tred to the great; the great who trod our fa-thers down, who steal our chil-dren's bread, whose hands of greed are stretch'd to rob the liv-ing and the dead. Then we'll sing a re-bel song As we proud-ly sweep a long to end the age old ty-ran - ny that makes for hu-man tears and the march is near - er done with each set-ting of the sun and the ty-rant's might is pass-ing with the pass-ing of the years.

Continued overleaf

We sing no more of wailing
And no songs of sighs or tears
High are our hopes and stout our hearts
And banished all our fears
Our flag is raised above us
So that all the world may see
'Tis labour's faith and labour's arm
Alone can labour free

Chorus

Out of the depths of misery
We march with hearts aflame
With wrath against the rulers false
Who wreck our manhood's name
The serf who licks the tyrant's rod
May bend forgiving knee
The slave who breaks his slav'ry's chain
A wrathful man must be

Chorus

Our army marches onward
With its face towards the dawn
In trust secure in that one thing
The slave may lean upon
The might within the arm of him
Who knowing freedom's worth
Strikes hard to banish tyranny
From off the face of earth

Notes page 42.

32. JAMES CONNOLLY

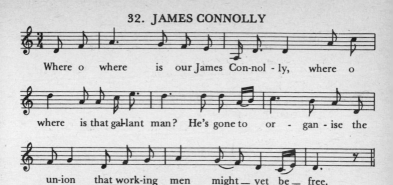

Where o where is our James Con-nol - ly, where o
where is that gal-lant man? He's gone to or - gan - ise the
un-ion that work-ing men might — yet be — free.

Where oh! where is the citizen army
Where oh! where are those fighting men
They have gone to join the great rebellion
To smash the bonds of slavery

And who'll be there to lead the van
Oh who'll be there to lead the van
Who should be there but our James Connolly
The hero of each working man

Who carries high that burning flag
Who carries high that burning flag
'Tis our James Connolly all pale and wounded
Who carries high our burning flag.

They carried him up to the jail
They carried him up to the jail
And there they shot him one bright May morning
And quickly laid him in his grave

Who mourns now for our James Connolly
Who mourns for that fighting man
Oh lay me down in your green garden
And make my bearers union men

We laid him down in yon green garden
With union men on every side
And swore we'd make one mighty union
And fill that gallant man with pride

Now all you noble Irishmen
Come join with me for liberty
And we'll forge a mighty weapon
And smash the bonds of slavery. *Notes page 42.*

The man was all shot through that came to-day
Into the barrack square;
A soldier I — I am not proud to say
We killed him there;
They brought him from the prison hospital:
To see him in that chair
I thought his smile would far more quickly call
A man to prayer

Maybe we cannot understand this thing
That makes these rebels die
And yet all things love freedom — and the spring
Clear in the sky
I think I would not do this deed again
For all that I hold by;
Gaze down my rifle at his breast — but then
A soldier I

They say that he was kindly — different too,
Apart from all the rest;
A lover of the poor; and all shot through,
His wounds ill drest
He came before us, faced us like a man,
He knew a deeper pain
Than blows or bullets — Ere the world began;
Died he in vain?

Ready — present; And he just smiling — God
I felt my rifle shake
His wounds were opened out and round that chair
Was one red lake
I swear his lips said "fire" when all was still
Before my rifle spat
That cursed lead; and I was picked to kill
A man like that.

Notes page 43.

34. THE PEAT-BOG SOLDIERS

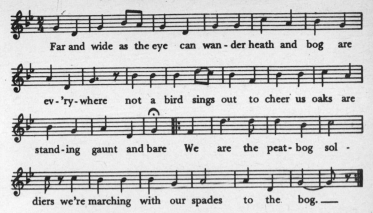

Far and wide as the eye can wan-der heath and bog are ev-'ry-where not a bird sings out to cheer us oaks are stand-ing gaunt and bare We are the peat-bog sol-diers we're marching with our spades to the bog.

Up and down the guards are pacing
No one, no one can get through
Flight would mean a sure death — facing
Guns and barbed wire greet our view

Chorus

But for us there is no complaining
Winter will in time be past
One day we shall cry rejoicing
Homeland dear, you're mine at last!

Chorus

Then will the peat-bog soldiers
March no more with their spades to the moor

Notes page 44.

95

35. BANDIERA ROSSA

The peo-ple on the march the road are tread-ing that leads to free-dom that leads to free-dom the hour of strug-gle's here our cour-age need-ing our ban-ner lead-ing to vic-to-ry.

Chorus:
Raise then the scar-let flag tri - umph-ant - ly Raise then the scar-let flag tri-umph-ant - ly Raise then the scar -let flag tri- umph-ant - ly We fight for peace and pro-gress and our lib - er - ty, op-press-ion shall cease.

From mines and factories, from farm and college
With strength of suffering and force of knowledge
Come all who hope for life, their power conceding
Our banner leading to victory.

Chorus

Away with enmities and hostile frontiers
To equal manhood the earth is bounteous
The rule of greed and war from earth is fading
Our banners leading to victory.

Chorus

Notes page 45.

96

36. JARAMA

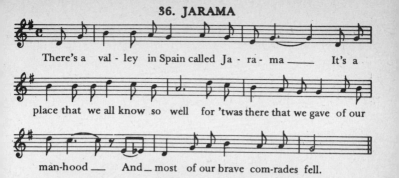

There's a val-ley in Spain called Ja-ra-ma ___ It's a
place that we all know so well for 'twas there that we gave of our
man-hood ___ And ___ most of our brave com-rades fell.

There's a valley in Spain called Jarama
It's a place that we all know so well
It was there that we fought the fascists
We saw a peaceful valley go to hell

Chorus
    From this valley you know we are going
    But don't hasten to bid us adieu
    Even though we lost the battle in Jarama
    We'll set this valley free

We are men of the Lincoln Brigade
We are proud of the fight that we made
We know that you people of the valley
Will remember our Lincoln Brigade
Chorus
You will never find peace with the fascists
You'll never find friends such as we
So remember that valley of Jarama
And the people that will set that valley free
Chorus
All this world is like this valley called Jarama
So green and so bright and so fair
No fascists can dwell in our valley
Nor breathe in our freedom's air.

Notes page 46.

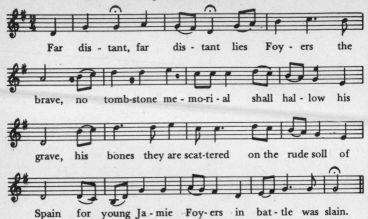

Far dis-tant, far dis-tant lies Foy-ers the brave, no tomb-stone me-mo-ri-al shall hal-low his grave, his bones they are scat-tered on the rude soil of Spain for young Ja-mie Foy-ers in bat-tle was slain.

He's gane frae the shipyard that stands on the Clyde
His hammer is silent, his tools laid aside
To the wide Ebro river young Foyers has gane
To fecht by the side o' the people o' Spain.

There wasna his equal at work or at play
He was strang in the union till his dying day
He was grand at the footba', at the dance he was braw
O! young Jamie Foyers was the floo'er o' them a'.

He cam' frae the shipyard, took off his working claes
Oh, I mind that time weel in the lang simmer days
He said: "Fare ye weel, lassie, I'll come back again"
But young Jamie Foyers in battle was slain.

In the fight for Belchite he was aye to the fore
He focht at Grandesa till he couldna fight more
He lay owre his machine-gun wi' a bullet in his brain
And young Jamie Foyers in battle was slain.

Notes page 46.

38. THE SUN IS BURNING

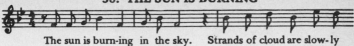

The sun is burn-ing in the sky. Strands of cloud are slow-ly

drif-ting by. In the park the dream-ly bees are dron-ing in the

flow'rs a-mong the trees and the sun burns in the sky.

Now the sun is in the west
Little kids lie down to take their rest
And the couples in the park are holding hands and waiting for
the dark
And the sun is in the west.

Now the sun is sinking low
Children playing know it's time to go;
High above a spot appears, a little blossom blooms and then
draws near
And the sun is sinking low.

Now the sun has come to earth
Shrouded in a mushroom cloud of death
Death comes in a blinding flash of hellish heat and leaves a
smear of ash
And the sun has come to earth.

Now the sun has disappeared
All is darkness, anger, pain and fear
Twisted sightless wrecks of men go groping on their knees and
cry in pain
And the sun has disappeared.

Notes page 49.

39. IF YOU MISS ME AT THE BACK OF THE BUS

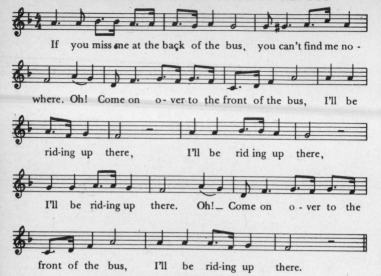

If you miss me at the back of the bus, you can't find me no-
where. Oh! Come on o-ver to the front of the bus, I'll be
rid-ing up there, I'll be rid ing up there,
I'll be rid-ing up there. Oh!— Come on o-ver to the
front of the bus, I'll be rid-ing up there.

If you miss me on the picket line
You can't find me no where Oh! Oh!
Come on over to the city jail
I'll be roomin' over there,
I'll be roomin' over there
I'll be roomin' there Oh! Oh! *etc.*

If you miss me in the Mississippi river
You can't find me no where Oh! Oh!
Come on over to the swimmin' pool
I'll be swimmin' right there
I'll be swimmin' right there
I'll be swimmin' right there Oh! Oh! *etc.*

If you miss me in the cotton field
You can't find me no where Oh! Oh!
Come on over to the court house
I'll be votin' right there
I'll be votin' right there
I'll be votin' right there Oh! Oh! *etc.*

Notes page 49.

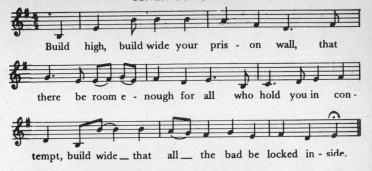

Build high, build wide your pris - on wall, that there be room e - nough for all who hold you in con - tempt, build wide _ that all _ the bad be locked in - side.

Though you have seized the valiant few
Whose glory casts a shade on you
How can you now go home with ease
Jangling your heavy dungeon keys

The birds who still insist on song
The sunlit stream still running strong
The flowers still blazing red and blue
All, all are in contempt of you

The parents dreaming still of peace
The playful children, the wild geese
Who still must fly, the mountains too,
All, all are in contempt of you

When you have seized both moon and sun
And jailed the poems one by one
And trapped each trouble-making breeze
Then you can throw away your keys

Notes page 49.

41. THE TIMES THEY ARE A-CHANGIN'

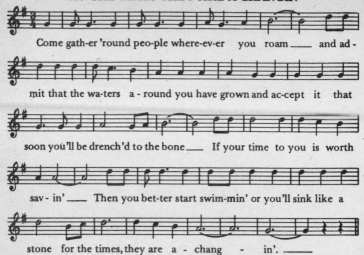

Come gath-er 'round peo-ple where-ev-er you roam ___ and ad-mit that the wa-ters a-round you have grown and ac-cept it that soon you'll be drench'd to the bone ___ If your time to you is worth sav-in' ___ Then you bet-ter start swim-min' or you'll sink like a stone for the times, they are a-chang - in'. ___

2. Come writers and critics
Who prophesise with your pen
And keep your eyes wide
The chance won't come again
And don't speak too soon
For the wheel's still in spin
And there's no tellin' who
That it's namin'
For the loser now
Will be later to win
For the times they are a-changin'

3. Come senators, congressmen
Please heed the call
Don't stand in the doorway
Don't block up the hall
For he that gets hurt
Will be he who has stalled
There's a battle outside
And it's ragin'
It'll soon shake your windows
And rattle your walls
For the times they are a-changin'

4. Come mothers and fathers
Throughout the land
And don't criticise
What you can't understand
Your sons and your daughters
Are beyond your command
Your old road is
Rapidly agin'
Please get out of the new one
If you can't lend your hand
For the times they are a-changin'

5. The line it is drawn
The curse it is cast
The slow one now
Will later be fast
As the present now
Will later be past
The order is
Rapidly fadin'
And the first one now
Will later be last
For the times they are a-changin'.
Notes page 49.

102

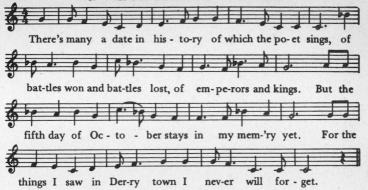

There's many a date in his-to-ry of which the po-et sings, of bat-tles won and bat-tles lost, of em-pe-rors and kings. But the fifth day of Oc-to-ber stays in my mem-'ry yet. For the things I saw in Der-ry town I nev-er will for-get.

Now poverty and hardship have long been Ireland's lot,
And some would say that Paddy's land is a place that's best forgot,
But I'm a true-born Derry man and I've never run away,
So with the few I joined the queue in the march that fateful day.

The Police came on like bully boys and told us we must cease,
For Derry town was not our own for marching where we please,
And wiser men and better men had given this advice,
And if we dared to disagree we would pay an awful price.

And then the gang advanced on us, the tyrants' hireling crew,
And smiling in their viciousness their sticks and batons drew,
On the 5th day of October I saw sights that warmed my brain,
The screams and shouts of injured men, and the awful cries of pain.

Oh! fools have ruled o'er men before, but always comes a time
Though beaten low by savage foe from off their knees they climb,
And woe be to the tyrants when the people's wrath is shown,
When corruption's laws and despot's cause are forever overthrown.

Come all you true-born working men and list awhile to me,
The 5th day of October will always precious be;
And freedom's torch that Derry lit will kindle far and wide
When the struggle's done and we've overcome, we can hold our head with pride.

Notes page 50.

43. THE MEN BEHIND THE WIRE

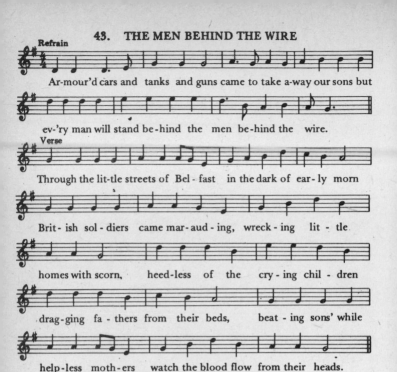

Refrain

Ar-mour'd cars and tanks and guns came to take a-way our sons but

ev'ry man will stand be-hind the men be-hind the wire.

Verse

Through the lit-tle streets of Bel-fast in the dark of ear-ly morn

Brit-ish sol-diers came mar-aud-ing, wreck-ing lit-tle

homes with scorn, heed-less of the cry-ing chil-dren

drag-ging fa-thers from their beds, beat-ing sons' while

help-less moth-ers watch the blood flow from their heads.

> Not for them a judge and jury
> Nor indeed a crime at all
> Being Irish means they're guilty
> So we're guilty one and all
> Round the world the truth will echo
> Cromwell's men are here again
> England's name again is sullied
> In the eyes of honest men *Chorus*
>
> Proudly march behind our banner
> Where we stand behind our men
> We will have them free to help us
> Build the Nation Once Again
> On the people step together
> Proudly firmly on your way
> Never fear and never falter
> Till the boys come home to stay *Chorus*
> Notes page 50.

104

44. THE TRAVELLERS' CAMPAIGN

Oh come all ye loyal travellers and listen to my song, although these words are sorrowful I will not keep you long. Sure it was in dear old Dublin as the snow came falling down. When the guards and corporation scabs came to burn our wagons down.

Oh it was in old Ballyfermot these brave travellers made their stand
Against those so-called Irishmen who were like Black and Tans
They attacked our camp one morning just at the dawn of day
Oh! what a shock they got my boys when they saw the old IRA

Now Peader O'Donnell he stood up that great man from Donegal
And they saw the anger in his eyes they fled aye, one and all
Those students too, God bless them, they did answer to our call
Saying: "We will come and camp with you, and with you we will fall."

Now our slogans they were printed, oh! how plainly they
could be seen
As we marched through dear old Dublin beneath our flag of
green
T'bould Connors and the Cashes and the Galvins were there too
Not forgetting Ginger O'Rourke and their leader Joe Donohue

Oh we heard of great St. Patrick and all he did for the Irish
Race
Now I wonder if he forgot to banish all the snakes
We pray to St. Columbus, he founded Amerikay,
And, please God, all in his own good time he'll find the
travellers a place to stay

Notes page 51.

45. BALLAD OF SHARPVILLE

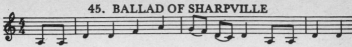

From the Cape to South-West A-fri-ca, from the Transvaal

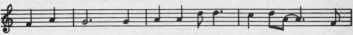

to the sea, in farm and vil-lage shan-ty-town __ The

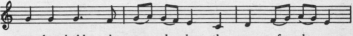

pass-law holds the peo-ple_down, the pass of_ sla-ve-

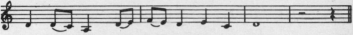

ry (Dom pass!) The_ pass_ of sla-ve-ry.

The morning wind blows through the land,
It murmurs in the grass;
And every leaf of every tree
Whispers words of hope to me:
"This day will end the pass." (Dom Pass!)
"This day will end the pass."

The sun comes up on Sharpville town,
And drives the night away,
The word is heard in every street,
Against the pass law we will meet,
No one will work today. (Dom Pass!)
No one will work today.

It was on the twenty-first of March,
The day of Sharpville's shame,
Hour by hour the crowd did grow,
One voice that cried the pass must go,
It spoke in freedom's name. (Dom Pass!)
It spoke in freedom's name.

Outside the police headquarter's fence,
The Sharpville people stand,
Inside the fence the white men pace,
Drunk with power and pride of race,
Each with a gun in hand. (Dom Pass!)
Each with a gun in hand.

The Sharpville crowd waits patiently,
They talk and laugh and sing.
At 11.15 the tanks come down,
Roll through the streets of Sharpville town,
To join the armoured ring. (Dom Pass!)
To join the armoured ring.

Neighbour talks to neighbour,
And the kids play all around,
Until without a warning word,
The sound of rifle fire is heard,
And men fall to the ground. (Dom Pass!)
And men fall to the ground.

The panic-stricken people run.
They flee the wild attack.
The police reload and fire again,
At running children, women, men,
And shoot them in the back. (Dom Pass!)
And shoot them in the back.

Sixty-Seven Africans
lay dead there on the ground,
(Apartheid's harvest for a day)
Three times their number wounded lay,
Their blood stained all around. (Dom Pass!)
Their blood stained all around.

There's blood on the men who fire the guns,
On the men who made the laws,
There's blood on the hands of the Whitehall ranks,
Who gave the thugs the guns and tanks,
Who help in Apartheid's cause.

Notes page 51.

APPENDIX 1
IMPORTANT EVENTS IN THE LIFE OF
JAMES CONNOLLY

1868   *June 5th* Born at Cowgate, Edinburgh. Third son of John Connolly (1833-1900) and Mary McGinn (1833-1892). Mrs. Connolly was from County Monaghan but it is not known what part of Ireland Connolly's father was from.

1878-81   Employed in printing works, bakery and mosaic tiling factory.

1882   Enlists in First Battalion, King's Liverpool Regiment. Probably served in Youghal, Castlebar, The Curragh, and Dublin.

1889   Leaves army.

April 13th Marries Lille Reynolds at Perth, Scotland. Now employed as carter by Edinburgh Cleansing Dept.

Active in socialist politics in Edinburgh as member of Socialist League and later The Scottish Socialist Federation (SSF). Succeeds his brother John as secretary of (SSF). Correspondent of Justice Journal of Social Democratic Federation (SDF).

1894   *November* Stands as socialist candidate for St. Giles Ward, Edinburgh, in municipal elections; Results: Liberal 1056 votes; Conservative 497 votes; Socialist (Connolly) 263 votes; Irish Nationalist 54 votes.

1895   *February* Sets up as a cobbler at 73 Buccieuch St., Edinburgh.

April Stands as socialist candidate in Poor Law election and is defeated by Monsignor Grady.

June Takes on full time work as socialist propagandist and organiser on recommendation of John Leslie who in *Justice* described Connolly as "a man among men". "No man has done more for the Socialist movement (in Edinburgh). If they have done as much certainly nobody has dared one half what he has dared in the assertion of his principles. He is the most able propagandist in every sense of the word that Scotland has turned out."

1896   *May* Becomes organiser of Dublin Socialist Club and goes to live at 76 Charlemont St., Dublin. (later moved to 54 Pimlico).

May 29th Appointed Secretary of Irish Socialist Republican Party (ISRP) at its foundation in the backroom of a public house in Thomas Street, Dublin.

	June 7th First Public meeting of (ISRP) at Custom House, Dublin.
1896	*September* Manifesto of ISRP issued from 67 Middle Abbey St. Gets work as labourer in Dublin Corporation.
1897	*June* Arrested following demonstration against Queen Victoria's Diamond Jubilee Celebrations. Lectures in Edinburgh. *December* Rank and file '98 Club founded by Connolly opened to General Public at meeting at 87 Marlborough Street, Dublin.
1898	*March 12th* Lectures in Dublin on Paris Commune. *March* Manifesto *The rights of life and the rights of property,* drafted by Connolly and Maud Gonne, issued as leaflet. Spends three weeks in Kerry reporting for *Weekly People* (New York) on famine. *June* Travels to Scotland to seek financial support for new ISRP paper. Kier Hardie loans £50. *August 13* First issue of *The Workers' Republic,* "A literary champion of Irish democracy, advocates an Irish Republic, the co-operative organisation of industry under Irish Representative Governing Bodies." *August 14* Lectures in Dublin on *Wolfe Tone and the Irish Social Revolution.*
1899	*February 14* Lectures at 21 Grattan Street, Cork, on *Labour and the Irish Revolution.* *May The Workers' Republic* reissued.
1900	ISRP sends delegates to International Socialist Congress in Paris. *October The Workers' Republic* reissued.
1901	*May-October* Lecture tour in Britain. *October* Delegate to Dublin Trades Council from United Labourers' Union. *November 13* Adopted at meeting in 71 Francis Street, Dublin, as Labour Candidate for Wood Quay Ward for Municipal Election.
1902	*January* Defeated in Municipal Election. Secures 431 votes against successful candidate's 1,424. *March The Workers' Republic* reissued. *May* Addresses May Day meeting held by Social Democratic Federation in Edinburgh. *August* Leaves for America on lecture tour as Representative of ISRP at invitation of Socialist Labour

110

Party. Begins campaign at the Copper Union, New York, by announcing: "I represent only the class to which I belong, and that is the working class."

September-December Lecture tour throughout United States from New York to Los Angeles. Visits Canada, contributes articles to *Weekly People* (New York) (Edited by Daniel De Leon) organ of the SLP.

1903   *January 2* Farewell meeting at Manhattan Lyceum Annex, New York. Returns to Dublin.

January Unsuccessful candidate for Wood Quay Ward in Dublin municipal elections. Secures 243 votes.

April Lecture tour in Scotland under auspices of Scottish District Council of SDF and later the *Glasgow Socialist Society.*

May A Rebel Song, set to music by Gerald Crawford, appears in May issue of *The Socialist* (Edinburgh).

June 7 Chairman at the inaugural meeting of Socialist Labour Party, Edinburgh, a breakaway from SDF. Later is appointed national organiser.

June-July Lecture tour in Scotland.

August Returns to Dublin. Addresses final open-air meetings in Foster Place of ISRP which proclaims itself the Irish section of the Socialist Labour Party.

September 18 Emigrates to America. Sets up residence in Troy, New York, working as an Insurance collector. Joins Socialist Labour Party.

1905   Active in *Industrial Workers of the World* (Wobblies) in Newark (New Jersey). Organises Singer factory in Elizabeth, New Jersey.

1907   *January* Member of National Executive Committee of Socialist Labour Party.

March 29 Irish Socialist Federation (ISF) founded at 79 Macdougal Street, New York. Member of founding committee.

October Resigns from Socialist Labour Party. (Date given by Desmond Ryan is April 1908).

Organiser of building section of New York Industrial Workers of the World. Completes *Labour in Irish History.*

1908   Found IWW Propaganda leagues at McMahon Hall, New York. Inaugural speech published in *Industrial Union Bulletin of IWW.* ISF *Manifesto to Irish Wageslaves* published in *New York Evening Call,* (organ of Socialist Party of America).

July Lecture tour of United States. Takes part in campaign of Eugene Debs for President. Delegate to fourth IWW convention in Chicago.

December Socialism made easy published in Chicago. Headquarters of ISF transferred to Chicago.

1909   *June* Appointed national organiser of Socialist Party of America and assigned to Middle West.

1910   *January The Harp* published from the office of *The Nation*, Dublin (Connolly, Editor, with Jim Larkin, Dublin Editor).

March Larkin initiates appeal for funds to bring Connolly on lecture tour to Ireland.

June-July Takes part in free speech campaign in New Castle, Pennsylvania, led by Big Bill Haywood. Edits *New Castle Free Press* when editor is jailed.

June Final issue of Harp.

July 14 Farewell banquet to Connolly at Cavanagh's Restaurant, New York.

July 26 Connolly arrives at Derry.

July 27 Visits Larkin in Mountjoy Prison, Dublin.

July 28 Reception at Antient Concert Rooms, Great Brunswick Street, Dublin.

August 7 Speaks at Custom House steps in Belfast.

August Joins Socialist Party of Ireland. Establishes branches in Belfast and Cork. Campaigns for Larkin's release from jail. *Labour, Nationality and Religion* published.

October Manifesto of SPI issued.

Campaigns with Maud Gonne McBride for extension to Ireland of the act providing for meals for school children. Appointed national organiser of SPI.

1911   *March* Moves to Belfast and joins Irish Transport Workers' Union. Issues manifesto on occasion of visit of King George 5th to Dublin.

July Appointed secretary and Ulster District organiser of ITWU with offices at 122 Corporation Street, Belfast. Living at Glenalina Terrace.

1911   *July* Addresses mass meeting of locked-out coal trade workers in Dublin.

October Leads millgirls' strike in Belfast.

November Founds Textile Workers section of ITWU (Mrs Tom Johnson first secretary). Delegate from ITWU to Belfast Trades Council

1912   *January 30* Arrives in Wexford to lead strikers and locked-out workers following arrest of P. T. Daly.
February Wexford strike settled. Cruise O'Brien, Editor of *Wexford Free Press,* acting as intermediatry between Connolly and employers.
Easter Conference organised by Connolly in Antient Concert Rooms, Dublin. Established Independent Labour Party of Ireland (ILP) "as the political weapon of the Irish working class". Programme drafted by Connolly.
April Home Rule Bill introduced in the House of Commons. Belfast Branch of ILP (I) holds meeting in St. Mary's Hall, Belfast, at which Connolly moves a resolution damanding Proportional Representation, excision of proposal for a senate and suffrage for women.
May At annual meeting of Irish Trade Union Congress in Clonmel, as delegate from the Belfast ITWU, Connolly proposes that "the Independant Representation of Labour upon all public boards be, and is hereby, included amonst the objects of congress." Motion supported by Larkin and passed by 49 votes to 18.
November 23 Issues manifesto *To the linen slaves of Belfast.*
Debates with Hilaire Belloc at Irish Club in London.

1913   *January* Contests Dock Ward in Municipal Elections in Belfast, supported by Trades Council. Secures 905 votes against Unionist opponent's 1,523.
March Issues *Ultimatum to the Linen Lords.*
May Delegate from ITWU to annual meeting of Irish TUC in Cork.
August 36 Tramway strike led by Larkin begins in Dublin.
August 29 Connolly speaks with Larkin at mass meeting outside Liberty Hall.
August 30 Connolly arrested. Refuses to give bail to be of good behaviour and is sentenced to three months imprisonment.
August 31 Bloody Sunday in Dublin. Police attack crowds in O'Connell Street.
September 1 TUC meeting in Manchester passes resolution demanding freedom of assembly in Dublin. Kier Hardie visits Connolly in Mountjoy Prison.

113

September 7 Goes on hunger strike.

September 14 Lord Lieutenant orders release.

September Returns to Belfast and is met by demonstration of dockers and millgirls led by labour band.

September 27 Connolly welcomes to Dublin the Steamship Hare, loaded with CWS Food paid for by TUC from Manchester.

October Connolly prepares statement of workers' case for Board of Trade Enquiry presided over by Sir George Askwith. Tours Scotland seeking support for Dublin workers.

October 27 Larkin convicted and lodged in Mountjoy Prison.

November Organises campaign for Larkin's release.

November 12 Issues manifesto to British working class and declares that until Larkin's release no ship will leave Dublin.

November 13 Larkin released. Larkin and Connolly draft appeal to British workers calling for a general strike.

November 14 Larkin leaves for Britain on *Fiery Cross* campaign. Connolly at Liberty Hall asks: "Why should we not drill and train men as they are doing in Ulster?"

November Speaks with Larkin at monster meeting in Free Trade Hall, Manchester, in support of Dublin workers.

November 19 Speaks at Albert Hall, London, with Larkin, George Lansbury, George Russell (A.E.), George Bernard Shaw, Sylvia Pankhurst.

November 23 Name *Citizen Army* first used officially.

1914 *January 4* Speaks at funeral of Alice Brady, a girl shot by a scab.

March 14 Denounces in *Irish Worker* proposal to partition the country.

March 22 Irish Citizen Army re-organised and constitution adopted.

April 17 Organises protest meeting against the proposed partition in St. Mary's Hall, Belfast.

June 1 Irish TUC meets in Dublin and becomes Irish TUC and Labour Party. Connolly elected to National Executive committee. Proposes motion (passed with three dissentients) condemning partition.

July 5 Speaks in Limerick at demonstration in support

of striking members of United Carmen's and Storemen's Society.

August In *Irish Worker* denounces the war. Issues manifesto under name of Irish Citizen Army, Belfast Division.

October Becomes President of Irish Neutrality League.

October 24 Larkin goes to America. Connolly becomes acting general Secretary of ITGWU editor of *Irish Worker* and Commandant-General of Irish Citizen Army.

December 5 Last issue of *Irish Worker* before its suppression.

1915   *May 29 The Workers' Republic* issued.

May 30 Addresses Labour Day demonstration in Phoenix Park.

July 18 Addresses anti-conscription meeting outside Liberty Hall.

December 14 Speaks at all-Ireland rally against conscription at Mansion House, Dublin.

1916   *January 19-22* Meeting with Military Council of Irish Republican Brotherhood, at which the date for rising is agreed (Easter Sunday, April 23). Becomes member of military council.

March 24 Police raid on Liberty Hall successfully resisted by Citizen Army.

March 26 A play *Under Which Flag*, by Connolly, performed in Liberty Hall by Workers' Dramatic Society.

April 16 "Green Flag of Ireland" raised over Liberty Hall.

April 23 Military Council of IRB meets in Liberty Hall and decides on rising on Easter Monday. Proclamation of Republic printed in basement of Liberty Hall.

April 24 Appointed Vice-President of the Provisional Government of the Irish Republic.

April 27 Connolly wounded. Shot in arm and then in ankle.

April 29 Surrender of Insurgent Forces. Connolly taken to Dublin Castle.

May 9 Court-Martialled and sentenced to death.

May 12 Strapped to a chair, is executed in Kilmainham Jail, Dublin.

APPENDIX 2

WRITINGS OF JAMES CONNOLLY

1896   *The Rights of Ireland* and *The Faith of a Felon*. This pamphlet originally written by James Fintan Lalor (1807-1849) was edited by James Connolly and published in Dublin.

1896   *October* First major political essay *Ireland for the Irish* published in three parts in *Labour Leader* (London).

1897   *Erin's Hope: The End and the Means.* Published by Irish Socialist Republican Party it contains articles originally published in *Labour Leader* and *Shan Van Vocht*, two newspapers published in London and Belfast respectively. A second edition issued as *Workers' Republic Pamphlet No. 1* (Believed by P. S. O'Hegarty to have been published in 1898) contains a poem entitled *Erin's Hope*, "written on reading comrade James Connolly's Pamphlet" by Mary M. Johnson, Detroit. An American edition with a preface by Connolly was published in New York in February 1902.

1897   *98 Readings.* Five pamphlets issued at fortnightly intervals, edited by James Connolly.
The Workers' Republic. A newspaper edited and largely written by James Connolly published in Dublin from August 1898- May 1903 in 85 issues (not continuous).

1901   *Home Thrusts* by Spailpín.

1901   *The New Evangel.* A reprint of essays originally published in *The Workers' Republic.*

1901   *Socialism and Nationalism.*

1907   *Songs of Freedom.* Published in New York.

1908   *The Harp.* Newspaper edited by James Connolly published monthly (1908-1910) in New York.

1909   *Socialism Made Easy.* Published by C. S. Carr and Co. Chicago. This first edition contains extracts from *Talking Points* originally published in *The Workers' Republic* in four articles. In 1911 the articles were incorporated into the Yearbook of the "One Big Union" movement in Australia under title of *The Axe to the Root.* The first European edition was published by The Socialist Labour Press, Glasgow in 1917.

1910   *Labour, Nationality and Religion.* Being a discussion
        of The Lenten Discourses against socialism delivered
        by Father Kane, S.J. in Gardiner Street Church,
        Dublin 1910. Published in *The Harp* Library Dublin.
        Labour in Irish History. The first general history of
        Ireland written from a Marxist standpoint. Chapters
        had originally been published in *The Workers' Republic*
        and *The Socialist* and *The Harp* (published in Dublin,
        Edinburgh and New York respectively). It was pub-
        lished by Maunsel and Co. Dublin.

1914   *The Irish Worker.* Connolly became editor of this
        weekly newspaper in succession to James Larkin who
        had founded the paper in June 1911. Published 24
        October-5 December until it was suppressed. One other
        issue was published on the 19th December 1914 under
        the title *Irish Worker.* Connolly went to Glasgow and
        had another paper printed there. *The Worker* published
        December 1914-January 1915 until it was also *sup-
        pressed* on February 20th, 1915.

1915   *The Workers' Republic.* Printed and published at Liberty
        Hall, Dublin. *Labour in Irish History* and *The Re-
        Conquest of Ireland,* were reprinted in one volume in
        1917 by Maunsel and Co., Dublin with an introduction
        by Robert Lynd, under the title *Labour in Ireland.*
        Further editions with the same title were published by
        Maunsel and Roberts Ltd., Dublin and London in
        1922 and by the ITGWU in 1944.

1918   *The Legacy and Songs of Freedom.* Published by the
        Socialist Party of Ireland, Liberty Hall, Dublin. Con-
        tains a Prefatory Poem by Maeve Cavanagh. The verses
        included are: A Legacy — the Dying Socialist to His
        Son; The Message; Arouse; A Rebel Song; Freedom's
        Pioneers; The Flag; A Festive Song; Saoirse A Rúin;
        The Watchword; Freedom's Sun; Be Moderate; Hymn
        of Freedom; The Call of Erin; When Labour Calls;
        Shake out your Banners; Oh! Slaves of Toil; A Father
        in Exile; Human Freedom.

        James Connolly also wrote two plays, *The Agitator's
        Wife,* written in The United States, and *Under Which
        Flag,* a Three-Act Play performed in Liberty Hall by
        The Worker's Dramatic Company on 26th March
        1916.

APPENDIX 3

IMPORTANT EVENTS IN THE LIFE OF JIM LARKIN

1876   Born on January 21st in Liverpool of Irish parents.

1887   Went to first job at 11 years. Before he was 16 had worked at various jobs. At 16 was a docker.

1893   Joined Independent Labour Party. Shipped out to Montevideo as a stowaway, worked as seaman, returning to Liverpool 1894.
Worked in Liverpool as Foreman Dock Porter involved in Socialist activity. Helped elect J. W. T. Morrissey, the first Socialist elected to Public Office in Liverpool. Arrested several times for street corner denunciations of the Boer War.

1901   Joined the National Union of Dock Labourers (NUDL).

1903   *September 8* Married Elizabeth Brown.

1905   *September* Elected to strike committee by Liverpool Dockers. Appointed temporary organiser of NUDL. This appointment was soon made permanent.

1906   Appointed General Organiser of NUDL. Reorganised most of Scottish ports where the branches had become moribund.

1907   Appointed to a Parliamentary Committee set up to examine piece work wages in dock labour. Organised Belfast Dockers and led strike of dockers in June. This strike developed into a general strike.
August 11 Formed Branch of NUDL in Dublin.

1908   Was at this time the father of two sons, James and Denis, living in Liverpool.
April Attended conference of Independent Labour Party as Delegate of Dublin Branch.
June Attended his second Irish Trades Union Congress (ITUC) as Delegate of Belfast NUDL. Elected to Executive of ITUC. Moved his family and set up home in Dublin. During this time involved in many strikes and disputes in different parts of Ireland.
December 7 Suspended by executive of NUDL who were not pepared to continue sanctioning strikes in Ireland.

1909   *January 4* Founded Irish Transport and General Workers Union (ITGWU). Elected first General Secretary.

August 18 **Arrested and charged with Conspiracy to Defraud the NUDL.** This was because money sent by Cork workers to aid the Dublin Carters in November-December 1908 had been distributed to the carters on strike and had not been entered in the books of the NUDL.

1910   *June* Trial opened in Dublin. Larkin found guilty. Sentenced to 1 year hard labour.

        October 1 Released from prison.

1911   Founded and edited *The Irish Worker* and *People's Advocate*, a weekly news paper which was very popular in June. The circulation was 26,000 copies, in August 74,750, in September 94,994. This leveled off to 20,000 per week.

        June Elected to Executive of ICTU.

        June 14 2,000 coalmen locked out. Dispute settled successfully by Larkin with wage increases.

1912   *January 3* Selected as Local Authority Candidate by Dublin Labour Party. In the subsequent election 5 of the 8 Dublin Labour Party candidates including Larkin elected.

        March Sued for his seat on grounds of being a convicted felon and barred for sitting for 5 years. After a court case this was increased to 7 years.

1913   *March* Settled successfully strike in City of Dublin Steam Packet Co.

        May Secured wage increases for Port workers.

        August 3 Rented Croydon House and 3 acres of land at Clontarf for use as recreation centre for members of ITGWU.

        August Secured wage increases for rural workers in Co Dublin.

        August 26 Calls strike of tramwaymen in Dublin in protest against dismissals.

        August 28 Larkin arrested for seditious Libel and Conspiracy. Released on bail.

        August 31 Addresses mass meeting from window of Imperial Hotel. This was followed by savage baton charges. Larkin arrested.

        September 3 404 Dublin employers decide to lock-out all ITGWU members.

        September 12 Released from jail.

        September 14 Addresses mass meeting in Manchester.

September 15 Returns to Dublin.

September 21 Addresses mass meeting in Glasgow.

September 22 Attends meeting in London of National Transport Workers Federation. British Trade Union Congress (BTUC) votes £5,000 to Dublin men. During the Dublin lock-out the BTUC raised £93,637.

September 27 Supervised unloading of First Food Ship *Hare* at Dublin.

October 2 Represents workers' viewpoint, and cross-examines at Official Government Inquiry into dispute.

October 3 Cross-examines William Martin Murphy.

October 6 Magnificently presents workers' case to inquiry.

October 10 Speaks in London.

October 27 Sentenced to 7 months without hard labour for his attempted "Bloody Sunday" speech.

November 11 Released from prison. Announces his intention of going on a *Fiery Cross* campaign to England, Scotland and Wales to raise funds and support for Dublin workers.

November 13 Larkin and Connolly issue joint manifesto.

November 15 Addresses mass meeting in Manchester.

November 19 Addresses meeting in London.

November 21 Issues manifesto to rank and file trade unionists.

November 23 Addresses meeting in Cardiff.

November 24 Addresses meeting in Bristol.

November 25 Addresses meeting in Sheffield.

November 30 Addresses meeting in London.

December 1 Addresses meeting in Liverpool.

December 2 Addresses meeting in Leicester.

December 9 Addresses BTUC special congress in London.

1914 *February 11* BTUC officially closes Dublin Relief Fund.

February 14 Announces plan for a Co-operative Commonwealth.

February-March Undertakes extensive speaking tours in England to raise funds for badly hit ITGWU.

June 1 Was Chairman of Annual ITUC in Dublin.

October 24 Farewell message to Citizen Army printed in *Irish Worker*.

October Sailed to America for lecture tour to raise funds for ITGWU.

November Gives interview to *New York Call* expounding anti-war views.

November 8 Addresses mass meeting of 15,000 in Madison Square Garden called to celebrate election victory of Socialist Congressman Meyer London.

November Addresses meeting to commemorate manchester Martyrs.

December Forms *Four Winds Fellowship*, an organisation of socialists born in the British Empire pledged to oppose Britain during the War.

1915   *Early part of Year* Addressed various socialist and other bodies but was not very successful in raising funds. He lived in almost poverty. Lecture Tours on West Coast.

September Forced to take a job. Undertook organising campaign for *Western Federation of Miners*.

November 15 Was speaker at funeral of executed Joe Hill, an IWW member.

1916   *May 21* Organised mass meeting in Chicago in support of Dublin insurrection.

Óctober Brought out American edition of *Irish Worker*.

November Spoke at election meetings for Eugene Debs, Socialist Candidate for Congress.

1917   *June* Arrested for speaking against conscription. The charges were dismissed.

August Joined American Socialist Party. Through all of this time he was working in some ways for German Intelligence to frustrate American aid to Britain and involvement in the War.

1918   Maintained contacts with Dublin Trade Union leaders and expressed desire to return to Ireland. Member of *James Connolly Socialist Club* in New York.

Main speaker at a rally organised by Socialist Party in support of Russian Revolution.

Spoke at many rallies for this purpose.

Spoke at rallies to raise funds for mass trials of IWW members.

1919   *February 2* Main speaker at memorial meeting in Boston for Carl Liebknecht and Rosa Luxembourg. This was part of a *Red Week*. Elected to International Bureau of the Left, a group within the Socialist Party.

February 15 Was elected to Executive of this body.

June 21 Attended a National Left Wing Conference in New York. Elected to National Council of the Left Wing.

August Again making efforts to return to Ireland.

September Joined Communist Labour Party on its foundation.

November 8 Larkin and about 500 other radicals arrested in New York.

November 10 Charged with Criminal Anarchy for his part in publishing *Left Wing Manifesto.* Held on 15,000 dollars bail.

November 20 Released on bail. Addressed meeting of communists and urged "the workers to spread the tidings of Communism".

1920   *April* Trial opens with Larkin defending himself.

May 3 Found guilty and sentenced to 5 to 10 years in Sing Sing Prison.

1921   *December 10* Issued Manifesto from prison supporting republican side in Civil War in Ireland.

1922   *January* Elected to membership of Moscow Soviet, USSR.

May 6 Released from prison. From The President of The Communist International Zinoviev he received a cablegram: "The Communist International sends its warmest greetings to the undaunted fighter released from The Democratic "Prisons".

July State court of appeal upheld his conviction and he was returned to Sing Sing.

1923   *January 17* Granted a free pardon and released. Went to see Secretary of Labour in Washington to demand his deportation.

April 30 Arrived in Dublin after deportation from America. Addressed meeting from window of Liberty Hall. (This was at the end of civil war). Urges "Peace, Reconstruction, Charity to All".

May 6 Addresses gigantic Labour Day commemoration in Croke Park. Addresses Connolly Commemoration Concert in Theatre Royal.

May 13 Speaks at meeting to mark the Seventh Anniversary of execution of James Connolly.

May 19 Begins two week tour of Union Branches in South of Ireland.

May 14 **Addresses Delegate Conference of ITGWU.**

June 3 Addresses No. 1 Branch of ITGWU in Dublin. This was a momentous meeting as it brought to a head differences between union leaders.

June 10 Addresses No. 1 and No. 3 branch and secures suspension of some members of the executive.

June 11 Larkin and supporters seize control of union offices and refuse to allow suspended members to enter. Union executive suspends Larkin. Launches again *Irish Worker* newspaper.

Legal action taken by Union Officers and Executive to establish that they were the legal trustees, officers and executive committee of Union.

September Founded *Irish Workers' League*

1924   *February 20* Legal actions determined in favour of union executive.

March 14 Expelled from ITGWU. 45 of Larkin's supporters arrested in Liberty Hall charged with unlawful occupation, sentenced to 1 month in jail.

Early June Invited by Communist International (Comintern) to represent Ireland at the fifth congress in Moscow on June 17. Arrived at Leningrad. Spoke at sessions of Comintern.

June 15 Larkin's brother launches *Workers Union of Ireland.* Two thirds of Dublin membership of ITGWU joins up.

July 8 Larkin elected to Executive Committee of Communist International.

July 11 Addressed the Third Congress of Red International of Labour Unions (Profintern).

July Spoke at sessions of Profintern.

August 25 Returns to Dublin. Addressed gigantic welcome home procession followed by meeting in Mansion House.

Government passes *Public Safety Act.* Larkin addresses meeting from window of Unity Hall Headquarters of Workers Union of Ireland (WUI) to protest against the "Tzarist Methods" of the government. Addresses delegates of Irish Workers' League (IWL). IWL decide to contest 3 Dublin Dáil seats in General Election.

September Larkin elected in North Dublin. Son James elected in County Dublin. Larkin prevented from taking his seat because he was an undeclared bankrupt for not having paid costs in legal action lost to Executive of ITGWU in February 1924.

1928   *February* Attended Executive meetings of Comintern. Addressed Moscow Soviet.

1932   *Early February* Contested North Dublin unsuccessfully. *March 19 Irish Worker* collapses due to lack of funds.

1933   *January* Contested North Dublin again unsuccessfully. Lost his seat on Dublin Municipal Council (Corporation).

1936   *Summer* Regained his seat on The Dublin Council.

1937   *July 4* Won Dáil seat for North East Dublin.

1938   *June* Lost his Dáil seat in General Election.

1941   *December* Larkin and son James joined Irish Labour Party.

1942   Was Official Labour Candidate in Municipal Elections, was re-elected. Labour became largest party in Council.

1943   *June* Wins Dáil seat in North-East Dublin. Son James wins seat in South Dublin.

1944   Loses his seat in General Election.

1946   Shortly before Christmas, while inspecting repairs in Union Hall, he slipped and injured himself internally.

1947   *Early January* Admitted to Meath Hospital. *January 30* Died in his sleep aged 71. *February* Buried in Glasnevin.

BIBLIOGRAPHY
Asterisk denotes book giving music

1. *An Anthology of Chartist Literature* J. W. Kovalyov (Moscow 1956).

2. Allan Thomas. *Allan's Tyneside Songs* (Frank Graham, Newcastle-Upon-Tyne, 1972.)

3. Aptheker Herbert *And Why Not Every Man.* The story of the fight against negro slavery. (Seven Seas Books, Berlin, 1961.)

4. Beauchamp Joan *Poems of Revolt.* A Twentieth Century Anthology (Labour Research Department 1969.)

5. Birch Lionel *The History Of The TUC 1868-1969. A Pictorial Survey Of A Social Revolution. (General Council Of The TUC, London 1970.)*

6. Bold Alan *The Penguin Book of Socialist Verse* (Penguin 1970.)

7. Boyd Andrew *The Rise Of The Irish Trade Unions 1729-1970.* (Anvil Books Ltd, Kerry, Ireland 1970.)

8. Boyle J. W. *Leaders And Workers.* (The Mercier Press, Cork, No Date.)

9. *Buchan Norman *101 Scottish Songs* (Collins, Glasgow and London 1964.)

10. *Carpenter Edward *Chants Of Labour* A Song Book Of The People. (Swan Sonnenschein and Co., London 1888).

11. Causley Charles *Modern Folk Ballads* (Studio Vista, London 1966).

12. *Chambers Robert *Songs Of Scotland Prior To Burns* (W. and R. Chambers, Edinburgh and London 1880).

13. Cole G. D. H. and Raymond Postgate *The Common people 1747-1946.* (Methuen and Co. Ltd., 1971.)

14. Connell Jim *Red Flag Rhymes* (The Agitators Press, Huddersfield and Labour Leader Glasgow. No date.)

15. Connolly James *Socialism and Nationalism* Edited by Desmond Ryan (At The Sign Of The Three Candles, Dublin 1948.)

16. *Labour and Easter Week 1916* Edited by Desmond Ryan (At The Sign Of The Three Candles, Dublin 1949.)

17. *The Workers' Republic* Edited by Desmond Ryan (At The Sign Of The Three Candles, Dublin 1951.)

18. *Labour In Ireland* (At The Sign Of The Three Candles. Dublin, no date.)

19. *Labour, Nationality and Religion* Being A Discussion

Of The Lenten Discourses Against Socialism Delivered By Father Kane S.J. in Gardiner Street Church 1910. (New Books Publications, 1962.)

20. *The James Connolly Songbook* (James Connolly Workers' Club, Dublin, no date.)

21. *Songs of Labour.* (New Books, Dublin and Belfast, 1954.)

22. *The Legacy and Songs Of Freedom* (The Socialist Party Of Ireland, no date.)

23. *Craig David "The Real Foundations"* literature and Social Change. (Chatto and Windus, London, 1973.)

24. Cronin Sean *The Rights Of Man In Ireland* (Wolfe Tone Society, Dublin, no date.)

25. *The Revolutionaries* (Republican Publications Ltd., Dublin, 1971.)

26. Daiken Leslie H. *Goodbye Twilight* Songs Of The Struggle In Ireland. (Lawrence and Wishart, London, 1936.)

27. Davis Angela *If They Come In The Morning* Voices Of Resistance. (Orgack and Chambers, London, 1971.)

28. Deasy Joseph *Fiery Cross* The Story Of Jim Larkin. (New Books Publication, Dublin, 1963.)

29. De Sola Pinto V. and A. E. Rodway. *The Common Muse.* Popular British Ballad Poetry from the 15th to the 20th Century. (Penguin Books 1965.)

Engels Frederick *see Marx, Karl.*

30. *Fagan H. and R. H. Hilton The English Rising of 1381* Lawrence and Wishart, London, 1950.)

31. Fitzhenry Edna C. *Henry Joy McCracken* (The Talbot Press Ltd., Dublin, 1936.)

32. Foner Dr. Philip S. *The Case Of Joe Hill* The story of the trial, the mass defence campaign, and the execution of the famous IWW poet, songwriter and organiser. (International Publishers, New York 1965.)

33. *The Letters Of Joe Hill* (Oak Publications, New York, 1965.)

34. Ford Robert *The Poetical Works And Letters Of Robert Burns* with Introduction, Notes and Glossary. (Collins, London and Glasgow, 1903.)

35. Fowke Edith and Joe Glaser *Songs Of Work and Protest* (Dover Publications Inc., New York, 1973.)

36. Fox R. M. *Jim Larkin: Irish Labour Leader* (International Publishers Inc., New York, 1957.)

37. *The History Of The Irish Citizen Army.* (James Duffy and Co. Ltd., Dublin, 1943.)

38. *Galvin Patrick *Irish Songs of Resistance 1169-1923* (Oak Publications, New York, 1962.)

39. Gammage R. G. *History Of The Chartist Movement 1837-1854* (Merlin Press, London, 1969.)

40. Gemkow Heinrich *Karl Marx — A Biography* Verlag Zeit im Bild, Dresden, 1968.)

41. *Gifford Alan *If I Had A Song.* A Song Book For Children Growing Up. (Workers' Mucic Association, London, 1954.)

42 Gilfellon Tom *Tommy Armstrong Sings* (Frank Graham, Newcastle-Upon Tyne, 1971.)
    Glaser Joe *see Fowke Edith.*

43. Gomez Manual *Poems For Workers — An Anthology.* (The Daily Worker Publishing Co, Chicago, no date.)

44. Greaves C. Desmond *The Life And Times Of James Connolly* (Lawrence and Wishart, London, 1961.)

45. *Theobald Wolfe Tone And The Irish Nation 1763-1973.* (Connolly Publications, London, 1963.)

46. *The Irish Question And The British People — A Plea For A New Approach* (Connolly Publications, London, 1963.)

47. *Greenway John *American Folksongs Of Protest* (Octagon Books, New York, 1971.)
    Harmon Frank *see Stavis Barrie*

48. Haywood William D. *The Autobiography Of Big Bill Haywood* (International Publisher, New York, 1969.)
    Hogan Robert *see O'Casey Sean*
    Hilton R. H. *see Fagan H.*

49. *Hogg James *The Jacobite Relics Of Scotland* (Edinburgh MDLCCXIX.)

50. Jackson George *Soledad Brother — The Prison Letters Of George Jackson* Penguin, 1971.)

51. Jackson T. A. *Ireland Her Own.* An Outline History Of The Irish Struggle For National Freedom And Independence. (Seven Seas Publishers, Berlin, 1970.)

52. *Kelly Stan *Liverpool Lullabies.* (Heathside — Sing, London, 1964.)

53. *Labour Party Songbook* (The Labour Party, London, 1955.)

54. Larkin Emmet *James Larkin — Irish Labour Leader 1876-1947* (A Mentor Book, The New English Library, London, 1969.)

55. Lenin V. I. *Lessons Of The Commune an In Memory Of The Commune.* (Progress Publishers, Moscow, 1969.)

56. Lindsay Jack and Edgell Rickword *Spokesmen For Liberty* A Record Of English Democracy Through Twelve Centuries. (Lawrence and Wishart, London 1941.

57. *Linger Erika Dr. *Essays In Honour Of William Gallagher.* Life And Literature Of the Working Class. (Humboldt Universitat, Berlin, 1966.)

58. *Lloyd A. L. *Folksong In England.* (Lawrence and Wishart, London 1967.)

59. *Come All Ye bold Miners* Ballads and Songs Of The Coalfields. (Lawrence and Wishart Ltd., London, 1952.)

60. *Lomax Alan *Hard Hittings Songs For Hard Hit People.* Notes on songs by Woody Guthrie. Music transcribed by Pete Seeger. (Oak Publications, New York, 1967.)

61. *Mac Coll Ewan *Folksongs and Ballads Of Scotland.* (Oak Publications, New York, 1965.)

62. *The Shuttle And Cage* Industrial Folk-Ballads. (The Workers' Music Association, 1954.)

63. *Personal Choice* Scottish Folksongs And Ballads. (Hargail Music Press, New York, 1963.)

64. *Mac Coll Ewan and Peggy Seeger *The Ewan Mac Coll-Peggy Seeger Songbook.* (Oak Publications, New York, 1963.)

65. *I'm A Freeborn Man* and Other Original Radio Ballads and Songs Of British Workingmen, Gypsies, Prizefighters, Teenagers, and Contemporary Songs Of Struggle and Conscience (Oak Publications, New York, 1968.)

66. *Songs For The Sixties* (Workers' Music Association, London, 1961.)

67, *The Singing Island* A Collection Of English and Scots Folksongs. (Mills Music Ltd., London, 1960.)

68. Mac Dermot Frank *Theobald Wolfe Tone and His Times* (Anvil Books, 1969.)

69. Mac Gabhann Liam *Rags, Robes And Rebels.* Poems Of Revolution. (Eibhlin Republican Press Ltd., Dublin, 1933.)

70. Mac Manus M. J. *Thomas Davis and Young Ireland.* (The Stationary Office, Dublin, 1945.)

71. Marx Karl and Frederick Engels *On Britain* containing *The Condition Of The Working Class In England.*

(Foreign Languages Publishing House, Moscow, 1962.)

72. *On the Paris Commune* (Progress Publishers, Moscow, 1971.)

73. *On Ireland* (Progress Publishers, Moscow, 1971.)

74. Mitchel John *The Jail Journal 1843-1853* (Browne and Nolan, Dublin, no date.)

75. Morton A. L. *A People's History Of England* (Lawrence and Wishart, London, 1968.)

76. Morton A. L. and George Tate *The British Labour Movement 1770-1920.* (International Publishers Inc., New York, 1957.)

77. Mulgan John *Poems Of Freedom* (Left Book Club, Victor Gollancz Ltd., London, 1938.)

78. Nevin Donal *1913 Jim Larking and The Dublin Lock-Out.*

79. Nolan Sean *1916-1966* Commemorative Booklet Issued By *The Irish Socialist*, April, 1966.

80. Norden Albert *Thus Wars Are Made* (Verlag Zeit im Bild, Dresden, 1970.)

81. Nowland Kevin B. *The Making Of 1916* Studies In The History Of The Rising. (The Stationery Office, Dublin, 1969.)

82. O'Casey Sean *Feathers From The Green Crow — Sean O'Casey 1905-1925.* Edited By Robert Hogan contains *The Story Of The Irish Citizen Army* (Macmillan and Co. Ltd, London, 1963.)

83. *O'Lochlainn Colm *Irish Street Ballads* Collected and Annotated by Colm O'Lochlainn and Adorned with Woodcuts From The Original Broadsheets. (The Three Candles Ltd., Dublin, 1962.)

84. **More Irish Street Ballads* Collected and Annotated By Colm O'Lochlainn and Adorned with Woodcuts from Various Sources. (The Three Candles Ltd., Dublin, 1956.)

85. *O'Shannon Cathal *Fifty Years Of Liberty Hall* The Golden Jubilee Of the Irish Transport And General Workers Union 1909-1959. (The Three Candles, Dublin, 1959.)

86. Palmer Roy *The Painful Plough* A Portrait Of The Agricultural Labourer In The Nineteenth Century From Folk Songs and Ballads and Contemporary Accounts. (Cambridge University Press, 1973.)

         ᵒtgate Raymond *see Cole G.D.H.*

87.   Prebble John *Culloden* (Penguin, 1961.)

88.   Raven Jon *Songs Of A Changing World* (Ginn and Co, London, 1972.)

89.   *Report Of The Commission On Itinerancy* (The Stationery Office, Dublin, 1963.)
       Rickword Edgell *see De Sola Pinto V.*

90.   Rolleston T. W. *Prose Writings Of Thomas Davis* (Walter Scott, London, 1889.)

91.   Ryan Desmond *The Rising.* The Complete Story Of Easter Week. (Golden Eagle Books, Dublin, 1966.)

92.   Ryan W. P. *The Irish Labour Movement* From The Twenties To Our Own Day. (The Talbot Press, Dublin, 1919.)

93.   Salt H. S. *Songs Of Freedom* (Walter Scott Publishing Co. Ltd., London and Felling-On-Tyne, 1906.)
       Seeger Peggy *see Mac Coll Ewan.*

94.   *Scott John Anthony *The Ballad Of America* The History Of The United States in Song And Story (Bantham Books Inc, New York, Toronto, London, 1966.)

95.   *Shannon Martin *Ballads From The Jails And Streets Of Ireland* (Red Hand Books, Dublin, 1966.)

96.   *Silber Irwin *Reprints From The People's Songs Bulletin 1946-1949* (Oak Publication Inc., New York, 1961.)

97.   *Lift Every Voice* The Second People's Songbook. Introduction by Paul Robeson (Oak Publications, York, 1957.)

98.   Sinclair Upton *The Cry For Justice* An Anthology Of The Literature Of Social Protest. The Writings Of Philosophers, Poets, Novelists, Social Reformers, and Others Who Have Voiced The Struggle Against Social Injustice. (Upton Sinclair, California, 1921.)

99.   *Songs Of The Workers* Issued July 1956. In Commemoration Of The 50th Anniversary Of The IWW. (Industrial Workers Of The World, Chicago, 1956.)

100.   *Spirit Of The Nation* Or Ballads and Songs By The Writers Of The Nation (James Duffy, Dublin, 1934.)

101.   *Stavis Barrie and Frank Harmon *The Songs Of Joe Hill* (Oak Publications, New York, 1960.)
       Tate George *see Morton A. L.*

102.   Thomas Hugh *The Spanish Civil War* (Penguin, 1968.)

103.   *Trade Union Information* (Irish Congress Of Trade

Unions Research Service, Dublin, Issue Of April 1968.)

104. West Julius *History Of The Chartist Movement* With An Introduction by J. C. Squire. (Constable and Co, London, 1920.)

105. Wright Robin *Poems Of Protest* (Studio Vista, London, 1966.)

106. *Winter Eric *And Since We're In Good Company* (Sing Publication, 1960.)

107. *Zimmermann Georges-Denis *Songs Of Irish Rebellion* Political Street Ballads And Rebel Songs 1780-1900. (Allen Figgis, Dublin, 1967.)

DISCOGRAPHY

1 *Songs of Joe Hill,* Joe Glazer (Folkways FA2039.

2 *Freedom Songs,* Paul Robeson (Topic TOP62).

3 *We Shall Overcome,* Pete Seeger (Columbia CL2101).

4 *Songs of The Spanish Civil War Vol. 1,* Pete Seeger and Ernst Busch (Folkways FH5436).

5 *Songs of The Spanish Civil War Vol. 2,* Woody Guthrie and Ernst Busch (Folkways FH5437).

6 *Songs of Protest,* The Ian Campbell Group (Topic TOP82).

7 *Folksound of Britain,* Jack Elliott (E.M.I. CLP1910).

8 *The Iron Muse,* Lou Killen (Topic 12T86).

9 *The Angry Muse,* Peggy Seeger and Ewan Mac Coll Argo ZDA83).

10 *The Jacobite Rebellions,* Ewan Mac Coll (Topic TPS114).

11 *Songs of Two Rebellions,* Ewan Mac Coll (Folkways FW8756).

12 *Songs of Robert Burns,* Ewan Mac Coll (Folkways FW8758).

13 *Topic Sampler Number 1,* The Ian Campbell Group (Topic TPS114).

14 *Al O'Donnell,* Al O'Donnell (Trailer LER2073).

15 *Joe Heaney,* Joe Heaney (Topic 12T91).

16 *100 Jahre Deutsches Arbeiter-Lied,* Various German Singers (Eterna 8010015A, 810016B).

17 *The Sun is Burning,* The Ian Campbell Group (Argo ZFB13).

18 *Songs of Irish Civil Rights,* Owen McDonagh (Outlet ZFB13).

19 *The Men Behind The Wire,* The Barleycorn (Andersonstown Civil Rights Committee CRC71).

20 *Jamie Foyers,* Ewan Mac Coll (Topic TRC55).

21 *New Briton Gazette Vol. 1,* Peggy Seeger, Ewan Mac Coll (Folkways FW8732).

22 *Moving On,* Nigel Denver (Decca LK4728).

23 *Talking Union,* Pete Seeger and The Almanac Singers (Folkways FW5285).

24 *Freedom Come All Ye,* The Exiles (Topic 12T143).

25 *The McKenna Brothers Live at O'Donoghue's,* The McKenna Brothers (Golden Guinea GGL0441).

26 *The Irish Rover,* Dominic Behan (Folklore F-LEVT-2).

27 *Saturday Night At The Bull and Mouth,* Peggy Seeger, Ewan Mac Coll (Blackthorne BR1055).

28   *Dark Horse On The Wind*, Liam Welden (Mulligan LUN 006).

29   *Contemporary Songs*, Peggy Seeger, Ewan Mac Coll (Folkways FW8736).

30   *Prosperous*, Christy Moore (Tara Tara 1000).

31   *The Iron Behind The Velvet*, Christy Moore (Tara Tara 2002).

32   *At The Present Moment*, Peggy Seeger, Ewan Mac Coll (Rounder Rounder 400).

33   *Tommy Armstrong of Tyneside*, Maureen Craik (Topic 12T122).

34   *Songs Of A Changing World*, Jon Raven, Nic Jones, Tony Rose (Trailer LER 2083).

35   *The Painful Plough*, Martyn Briggs, Roy Palmer, (Impact IMP-A103).

36   *Steam Whistle Ballads*, Ewan Mac Coll (Topic 12T104).

37   *Dangerous Songs*, Pete Seeger (Columbia CS9303).

38   *Songs Of Struggle And Protest*, Pete Seeger (Folkways FH5233).

39   *American Industrial Ballads*, Pete Seeger (Folkways FH5251).

40   *The Times They Are A Changing*, Bob Dylan (C.B.S. DPG62251).

41   *British Industrial Folk Songs*, Ewan Mac Coll (Stinson SLP79).

SOME SOURCES AND RECORDINGS

Note: Bib. = bibliography reference; Disc. = discography reference.

The Cutty Wren. Taken down early in the century by Miss Dorothy Blunt from the singing of Mr. Hawkins, an old shepherd of Adderbury West, Oxfordshire. Printed in A. L. Lloyd *The Singing Englishman.* (The Workers' Music Association, 1944.) Disc. 6, 13.

The Rocks of Bawn. Widely known traditional song of an agricultural worker's protest at his lot. Sung splendidly by Joe Heaney, Carna, Co. Galway. Disc 16.

Such a parcel of rogues. Printed in Bib. 49, p. 56, 57, and in Bib. 61. Disc 10, 11, 22.

Wae's me for Prince Charlie. One of the most beautiful of the Jacobite songs, still sung by traditional singers, notably Jim Christel of Dublin. Printed in Bib. 49. Disc 10.

La Marseillaise. The French National Anthem. Bib. 35.

Henry Joy. This popular Belfast ballad was written by T. P. Cuming and is printed by Fred Heatley in his fine book *Henry Joy McCracken* (Belfast Wolfe Tone Society. 1967.)

A man's a man for a' that. Written by Robert Burns. Bib. 34. Disc. 12, 24.

Skibbereen. An Anti-eviction ballad from the singing of Liam Welden of Dublin.

The West's Asleep. By Thomas Davis. Bib. 99.

The song of the lower classes. Written by Ernest Jones, the Chartist leader and printed in Bib. 10, p. 38, 39.

The Internationale. The most widely known of all Socialist songs. Disc 16.

The Red Flag. Written by Jim Connell and sung throughout the world. It is sung at the conclusion of all Annual Conferences of The British Labour Party.

The coal owner and the pitman's wife. The text of this ballad was communicated by J. S. Bell, of Whiston, Lancs., to the editor of *Coal* Magazine. Mr. Bell believed the ballad to have been written by William Hornsby, a collier of Shotton Moor. Bib. 59. Disc 8, 36.

The Durham lock-out. Words written by Tommy Armstrong. Bib. 59. Disc 33, 8.

The strike. Written by Joe Wilson, a printer and singer of Tyneside 1842-1875. Printed in *Joe Wilson Sings,* a collection of his best songs published by Frank Graham of New-castle Upon Tyne 1971. Bib. 8.

Fourpence a day. Collected by Joan Littlewood and Ewan Mac Coll from the singing of John Gowland, a retired lead miner of Middleton-In-Teesdale, Yorkshire. The song is attributed to Thomas Raine, lead miner and bard of Teesdale. Bib. 62. Disc. 36, 41.

The banks of the Dee. Communicated by J. White of Houghton-le-Spring, Durham, to the editor of *Coal* Magazine. Bib. 59. Disc. 7, 8.

William Brown. This ballad about over-production in the wood turning industry was written by Arthur Hagg and was printed in a songbook of the Independent Labour Party in 1927. Disc. 26.

My master and I. This song was written by Howard Evans and printed in his Songs for Singing at Agricultural Labourers' Meetings. Published in Roy Palmer's excellent book. Bib. 86. Disc. 35. Roy Palmer's other books will greatly reward the reader.

Solidarity forever. Written by Ralph Chaplin, an organiser of the Industrial Workers Of The World, in Jan. 1915. Sung to the tune *John Brown's Body.* Disc 23.

The Ludlow massacre. Written by Woody Guthrie. Bib. 94. Disc. 23.

Run to Jesus. American slave song, understood to be thinly disguised references to the free northern states. Bib. 47.

Oh! Freedom. Perhaps the best known of all freedom songs sung by Pete Seeger on his great album. Disc. 3.

My will. Written by Joe Hill. Bib. 33. Disc. I.

Casey Jones — The Union Scab. Another of Joe Hill's songs. Bib. 101. I, 37.

Joe Hill. Written in 1925 by Alfred Hayes and set to music by Earl Robinson. Bib. 35, 32. Disc. I, 2.

Dublin City. Odd verses of this ballad were written by the late Donagh Mac Donagh to be used in his play *Let Freedom Ring.* The ballad singer Ted McKenna was impressed greatly by the verses on Connolly and Larkin. It was his interest that caused the poet to complete the ballad. Disc. 25.

The Citizen Army. Written by Liam Mac Gabhann and published first in Michael Price's review, *Citizen Army* in 1935, The ballad is sometimes now sung to the same air as *The Foggy Dew.*

Jim Larkin RIP.. Author unknown. Bib. 84.

Be moderate. By James Connolly. Bib. 22.

A rebel song. The best known of James Connolly's Songs. Bib. 21.

James Connolly. Written by the playwright and singer from Cork, Patrick Galvin and printed in Bib. 38. Disc. 28, 14.

Connolly. By the poet-journalist Liam Mac Gabhann and first published in his collection *Rags, Robes and Rebels.* Bib. 69.

The peat-bog soldiers. Sung widely during the Spanish Civil War. Bib. 57. Disc. 4, 6, 16.

Bandiera Rossa. Popular Italian anti-fascist song. Disc. 4, 6, 16.

Jarama. Another song of the Spanish Civil War. Bib. 102. Disc. 4, 5.

Jamie Foyers. Written by Ewan Mac Coll Bib. Disc. 20.

The sun is burning. By Ian Campbell. Disc. 31, 17.

If you miss me at the back of the bus. A song born of the fight for de-segregation in America in the early sixties. Disc. 3.

In contempt. This song was written by Aaron Kramer and the tune by Betty Saunders. It was printed in the October 1950 issue of *Sing Out.* Bib. 94. Disc. 9.

The times they are a-changing. Words and tune by Bob Dylan. This song was enormously popular in the mid-sixties. Disc. 40.

The fifth day of October. Written by Owen Mac Donagh.

The men behind the wire. The introduction of Internment raised much anger. This song, by Pat McGuigan of Belfast, is an expression of that anger.

The Travellers' campaign. By Joe Donohue, sung to the air normally associated with *The Rocks of Bawn,* which is very popular with travellers. The song was printed as a broadsheet and sold in Dublin.

The ballad of Sharpville. The words and mustic of this powerful ballad were written by Ewan Mac Coll a few days after the events described therein. Bib. 65. Disc. 27.

Acknowledgements

I extend my warm thanks to David Fitzgerald who collaborated with me in the editorial work. His advice and encouragement was an inspiration, in addition to this he transcribed all the tunes for the book. Thanks also to Alfred Batch of The Workers' Music Association, Andrew Boyd, Donal Nevin, Fred Heatley, Ambrose Collins and Mrs I. Wagner of the British Labour Party Library for making source material available to me. I also thank for advice A. L. Lloyd, Seamus Geraghty, Tom Redmond and especially John Flood who helped at all stages. For help with typing and photocopying I thank Patricia Phelen, Carmel Curren, Celia Ennis, Brian Kelly and Bernadette McDonnell. My thanks are also due to the editors and authors of the books listed in the Bibliography, especially Ewan MacColl, A. L. Lloyd and Roy Palmer whose work I so greatly admire.

The editor and publisher gatefully acknowledge the assistance of *The Workers' Music Association*, London for songs 1 and 32; *A. L. Lloyd* and *Lawrence and Wishart*, London, for songs 13, 14 and 17; *Ginn & Co.*, *London* for song 15; *Ewan McColl* for songs 16, 37 and 45; *Cambridge University Press* for song 19; *Octagon Books*, New York, for songs 21 and 22; *Oak Publications*, New York, for songs 24, 25 and 40; *Mr Ted McKenna* for song 27; *Liam Mac Gabhann (RIP)* for song 28 and for his poem *Connolly* (number 33); *The Three Candles*, Dublin, for song 29; *Ian Campbell* for song 38; *Warner Bros. Music*, for song 41; *Outlet Records*, Belfast for song 42; *Mr Pat McGuigan*, and *Andersonstown Civil Resistance Committee*, Belfast, for song 43. *Full details of all these works are given in the section,* Some Sources and Recordings, *on page 134.*

SONGS OF BELFAST
David Hammond

From the richness of Belfast life David Hammond offers you this selection of songs, a tribute to all the generations who have made their home on the banks of the Lagan.

David Hammond was born and reared in Belfast. His interest in Irish music is known through his singing, his collections of songs from many parts of the island and his own records.

CEOLTA GAEL
Sean Og agus Manus O Baoill

The music and words to 92 Irish songs make up this collection. The words of each song are printed in the Irish language. Some of the more well-known titles include *Ar Eirinn ni Neosfainn Ce hI*, *An Raibh Tu ar an gCarraig?*, *Anach Cuan*, *Banchonic Eireann O*, *An Bunnan Bui*, *An Droighnean Donn*, *Eamon an Chnoic* and *Sliabh na mBan*.

BALLADS FROM THE PUBS OF IRELAND
Compiled by James N. Healy

A thoroughly enjoyable, roistering collection of sad songs, merry lyrics and ballads of love that people roar out with a depth of feeling in the pubs of Ireland.

ONE DAY IN MY LIFE
Bobby Sands.

One Day in My Life is a human document of suffering, determination, anguish, courage and faith. It also portrays frightening examples of man's inhumanity to man.

Written with economy and a dry humour it charts, almost minute by minute, a brave man's struggle to preserve his identity against cold, dirt and boredom. It is the record of a single day and conjures up vividly the enclosed hell of Long Kesh; the poor food, the harassment and the humiliating mirror searches. Bobby Sands and his comrades were often gripped by terror at the iron system that held them and yet their courage never faltered.

Written on toilet paper with a biro refill and hidden inside Bobby Sands' own body, this is a book about human bravery and endurance and will take its place beside the great European classics on imprisonment like *One Day in the Life of Ivan Denisovich* and our own John Mitchel's *Jail Journal.*

'I wish it were possible to ensure that those in charge of formulating British policy in Ireland would read these pages. They might begin to understand the deep injuries which British policy has inflicted upon this nation, and now seek to heal these wounds.'
From the Introduction by Sean MacBride.

SKYLARK SING YOUR LONELY SONG
An anthology of The Writings of Bobby Sands

This book paints a self-portrait of a remarkable man. Bobby Sands spent no less than nine of his short life of twenty-seven years in jail — and yet this book shows how well he could write. His 'Trilogy' has echoes of Wilde's *Ballad of Reading Gaol;* essays like 'I once had a Life' and 'I Fought a Monster Today' expound his political attitude and at the same time conjure up the day-by-day sufferings of Bobby Sands and his comrades in the H-Blocks — the bad food, the body-searches and the continual harassment. These writings mirror the struggle that won him a tragic fame throughout the world. He discusses the attitude of Irish politicians and the Catholic Church to the sacrifice being enacted by himself and his comrades. Most poignant of all, however, is 'The Lark', a beautiful parable of Sands' own long years of captivity that says 'I too have seen the outside of the cage.'

This book will appeal to the great mass of readers, whether they are interested in politics or not. Bobby Sands' defiant spirit shines through. A book to be enjoyed by anyone who admires courage, wit and eloquence in the face of Death itself.